The Pack Horse

A JOURNEY THROUGH THE SEASONS

LUKE PAYNE

©2023 Luke Payne &
Meze Publishing Limited

First edition printed in 2023 in the UK

ISBN: 978-1-915538-12-3

Written by: Luke Payne

Edited by: Katie Fisher & Phil Turner

Photography by: Dan Burns (naturalselectiondesign.com)

Additional Photography by: Rob Whitrow (robwhitrow.co.uk) (pages 5, 204, 205, 222, 223, 238, 239)

Designed by: Paul Cocker

Cover by: Dan Burns (naturalselectiondesign.com)

PR: Emma Toogood, Lizzy Capps

Contributors: Vicky Frost, Emily Retford, Kate McCann, Lis Ellis

Printed and bound in the UK by Bell & Bain Ltd, Glasgow

Published by Meze Publishing Limited
Unit 1b, 2 Kelham Square
Kelham Riverside
Sheffield S3 8SD
Web: www.mezepublishing.co.uk
Telephone: 0114 275 7709
Email: info@mezepublishing.co.uk

No part of this book shall be reproduced or transmitted in any form or by any means, electronic or mechanical, including photocopying, recording, or by any information retrieval system without written permission of the publisher.

Although every precaution has been taken in the preparation of this work, the publisher and author assume no responsibility for errors or omissions. Neither is any liability assumed for damages resulting from the use of this information contained herein.

CONTENTS

Foreword By Thom Hetherington	8
The Journey	14
A Note on the Recipes	28

Spring

Bowden Bridge & Hill Houses Walk	**32**
Wild Garlic Soup	38
Chicken & Wild Garlic Dumplings, Chicken & Wild Garlic Broth	40
Crab, Watercress Vichyssoise, Pickled White Asparagus	42
Asparagus, Poached Egg, Café de Paris Emulsion	44
St George's Mushrooms au Gratin, Wild Garlic Grissini	46
Rack of Lamb, Pressed Lamb Shoulder Potato, Pickled Morels	50
Beef & Pickled Walnut Stew, Nettle Dumplings	52
Turbot Poached on the Bone, White Asparagus, Morels, Sauce Bonne Femme	54
Breaded Whole Plaice, Mushy Peas, Chip Shop Curry Sauce	56
Jersey Royals Fried in Seaweed Vinegar, Purple Sprouting Broccoli, Lovage Pesto, Goat's Curd	58
Roast Lamb Leg with Anchovies, Capers, Rosemary & Mint	60
Wild Rabbit, Trotter & Mustard Pie	62
Chicken Ruby	64
Gin & Tonic Cheesecake, Cucumber Granita	68
Vanilla Crème Brulée, Pink Peppercorn Shortbread	70
Garden Rhubarb Crumble, Vanilla Custard	72
Chocolate & Peanut Butter Delice, Honeycomb, Blood Orange Ice Cream	74
A Day at The Pack Horse	**76**

Summer

Kinder Reservoir & Twenty Trees Walk	**84**
Isle of Wight Tomatoes, Burrata, Pickled Garlic Buds	92
Raw Courgettes, Fennel, Herbs, Pumpkin Seeds, Mozzarella	94
BBQ Mackerel, Gem Lettuce, Horseradish Ranch Dressing, Gooseberry Salsa	96
Charcoal Roast Octopus, Nduja Butter, Chimichurri	98
Smoked Haddock & Sweetcorn Chowder	100
Sea Trout, Samphire, Fennel, Butter Bean & Tomato Broth	104
Sole Grenobloise	106
Roast Noisette of Lamb, Cockles, Samphire, Salsa Verde	108
Traditional Roast Grouse, Damson Sauce	110
Harissa Roast Carrots, Pickled Carrots, Split Pea Purée, Carrot Top Dressing, Dukka	112
Herb Roast Chicken	114
Fish Pie	116
Côte du Boeuf, Peppercorn Sauce	118
Strawberries, Tarragon Ice Cream, Meringue, Verjus Syrup	122
Gooseberry & Elderflower Fool	124
Sea Buckthorn Posset, Heather & Almond Biscotti	126
Chocolate Fondant, Blackcurrant Ripple Ice Cream	128
Meet the Suppliers	**130**

Autumn

Mount Famine Walk	**136**
Manchester Egg	142
Beetroot Risotto	144
An English Autumn Porotos Granados	146
Scallops Baked in Seaweed Butter, Garlic & Thyme Crumb	148
Lamb Koftas, Sheep's Milk Labneh, Pickled Red Onion	150
Duck Breast, Confit Leg Spring Roll, Pickled Blackberries, Anise Carrots, Crispy Kale	154
Squirrel Ragout Pappardelle	156
Buffalo Ricotta Gnudi, Squash, Sage Butter, Walnut Pesto	158
Mussels Cooked in Beer with Bacon & Celeriac	160
Fish Stew	162
Roast Sirloin of Beef	164
Curried Goat Pie	166
Lamb Shoulder with Merguez Spices, Braised Fennel, Cucumber & Walnut Tarator	168
Lemon Cake	172
Heather Panna Cotta, Macerated Peaches	174
Greengage Clafoutis	176
Chocolate & Beetroot Brownies	178
Front of House at The Pack Horse	**180**

Winter

Lantern Pike Walk	**188**
Mushroom Ragout, Straw Potatoes, Pickled Walnut Dressing, Poached Eggs	194
Potato & Winter Truffle Soup	196
Crispy Ox Tongue, Winter Leaf & Lord of the Hundreds Caesar Salad	198
Chicken Liver Parfait, Farmhouse Chutney	200
Cured Trout, Buttermilk Beurre Blanc	202
Onion Squash Stuffed with Spelt, Mushrooms & Blue Cheese	206
Skrei Cod, Monk's Beard, Jerusalem Artichoke Purée, Golden Raisin Dressing	208
Grilled Halibut, Keralan Style Mussel Curry Sauce, Cauliflower Bhaji	210
Braised Pig's Cheeks, Trotter & Parsley Cream, Mustard Mash, Honey Roast Chicory	212
Venison Faggots, Celeriac Mash, Mushroom, Gherkin & Green Peppercorn Sauce	214
Roast Belly Pork with Fennel Seed Crackling	216
Truffle Dauphinoise, Caramelised Onion & Lincolnshire Poacher Pie	218
Venison Wellington	220
Red Wine Poached Pears, Cinnamon Buckwheat Crumb, Chantilly Cream	224
Salted Caramel Custard Tart	226
Poached Yorkshire Rhubarb, Ginger Cake, Rhubarb Syrup	228
Dark Chocolate Mousse, Stout Cake, Milk Ice Cream	230
Kinder Downfall Walk	**232**

Sunday Roast Sides

Perfect Roast Potatoes	242
Sunday Gravy Base	242
Yorkshire Puddings	243
Carrot & Swede Mash	243
Honey Roast Roots	244
Roast Savoy Cabbage & Caraway Butter	244
Creamed Spinach	245
Cauliflower Cheese	245

Stocks & Preserving

Chicken Stock	248
Beef Stock	248
Vegetable Stock	248
Fish Stock	249
Trotter Stock	249
Pickling Liquor & Brine	249

Breads & Pastry

Classic Shortcrust	250
Puff Pastry	250
Hot Water Pastry	250
Pasta Dough	251
Rosemary & Sea Salt Focaccia	251
Soda Bread	251

Curry Night Accompaniments

Onion Bhaji	252
Mint Yoghurt	252
Kachumber	253
Onion Seed Flatbread	253

Condiments

Tomato Ketchup	254
Mayonnaise	254
Aioli	255
Bread Sauce	255
Cucumber Relish	256
House Vinaigrette	256
Directory	**258**
Acknowledgements	**260**

FOREWORD BY THOM HETHERINGTON

A pub is a public house, in the most literal sense, and a gastropub is simply a public house with great food. Pubs, especially country pubs, should be as comfy as a slipper, offering a warm hug of familiarity and hospitality to all who cross the threshold. Drinkers and diners obviously, but such loose definitions should include families, cyclists, and those with muddy boots, or indeed muddy paws. Coincidently, each of these diverse demographics are welcomed by name on the painted panel by the front door of The Pack Horse in Hayfield. It's a good sign, in every sense.

Like all pubs, The Pack Horse has a history. In this instance, it is a long-established reputation for doing decent pub food. I live in the next town over and ate there many times over the decades, under a sequence of changing management, but as my food geekery escalated, my head and stomach were turned by the gastronomic fleshpots of Manchester and the Ribble Valley, so my patronage dropped off.

And that was that, until Autumn 2016 when a friend, journalist Kirstie McCrum, messaged to say new owners had taken on The Pack Horse and it was well worthy of an urgent return. By that point I had helped to launch Restaurant magazine and the 50 Best Restaurants in the World awards, written about the sector for trade and national press, and run my own hospitality exhibition, conference and awards for 12 years. I had my ear to the ground and my finger on the pulse. Could a pub of high ambition possibly have appeared in stealth mode, right under my finely attuned gastronomic nose?

Embarrassingly, it turns out that it could, and indeed it had.

Luke Payne and Emma Daniels, The Pack Horse's new owners, had bowled into the village out of nowhere. No pedigree to speak of, no trail of storied restaurants and kitchens on their CVs, and no clanking from sackfuls of industry awards to be heard as they moved in. This was simply a wild leap of faith on their part, from the safe drudge of small roles in big pubcos to the latent potential of this sleepy corner of the Pennines.

The gameplan, such as it was? To focus on sourcing fine ingredients, respectfully cooked and served with a genuine love of hospitality. They gave the place a frugal spruce and opened the doors.

As I sat at an outside table on my first visit to this latest iteration of The Pack Horse, I ate fine Cobble Lane charcuterie, excellent sourdough from a local artisan bakery, and for dessert, a hearty slice of humble pie. This, I instinctively (belatedly) knew, was going to be special.

And I stress that humble pie had never tasted so sweet – a beautiful short crust of hubris, pricked like an ego, encasing a rich filling of humility. I wanted to be wrong, more than anything, as this Northern tip of the Peak District, wild and bleak on the tops, mellow and lush in its sheltered valleys, had long been a gastronomic desert. As a local foodie, that both bruised my pride and limited my options.

So partly for those reasons of selfish altruism, and partly because Luke and Emma were so damn lovely and humble, I decided to help them in any way that I could. From this unofficial position of occasional advisor and unwavering advocate I've vicariously witnessed every step of their journey, every high and every low, and every crisis of confidence they've overcome.

There was the dilemma of dropping crowd-pleasing pub staples like burgers from the menu as the cooking became more fluid and finessed; the agonising over whether to invest in a more luxurious wine list to better suit the rising quality of food on the plate; the thickening of skin to the social media slings and arrows from the odd disgruntled guest who simply didn't get what they were doing or where they were going.

In the rear-view mirror these issues seem like mere bumps in the road, but at the time they were significant hills to be navigated, as ominous as scaling Kinder itself with a westerly storm blowing in.

Which brings me neatly to the landscape around Hayfield, which has informed so much of Luke and Emma's journey with The Pack Horse. Sourcing from local producers, such as Mettrick's for High Peak lamb or beers from Distant Hills Brewery, has defined their menus, but as incomers they've embraced the hills and seasons in every facet of their lives. I often bump into them tramping the lanes with their son Elliot in a pushchair and their dogs leading the way.

Such responsiveness to their surroundings is, I suppose, akin to the French concept of 'terroir', where the terrain and the weather shape what grows and thrives in any given location. Here, the terroir has produced a pub with a uniquely Peak District identity, so it feels only right that the hills and trails of the area, as well as the producers and their produce, are intertwined in this book alongside Luke's recipes.

Having built the pub of their dreams, the hope was that recognition would follow as surely as a pint follows a hike. And it has: a stellar review by the Sunday Times and a glowing write-up in the FT, as well as inclusion in the Michelin Guide, the Good Food Guide, and the esteemed 50 Best Gastropubs awards list. Local food writers have flocked and swooned, and most importantly countless first-time customers have become loyal regulars.

This success is their success – Luke and Emma's. Driven by them, delivered by their team, and deserved by all. This book, for which I am honoured to have provided the foreword, is a fine and timely summation of all they have achieved to date, but I have no doubt that it will only act as a launchpad for yet more to come.

Thankfully, this deluge of acclaim has changed both everything and nothing. There is still a pub quiz and a curry night; the bar still has finely kept local ales but also treats for dogs; there is serious cooking with pin-sharp techniques, but also easy bar food that keeps my teenaged boys happy. The Pack Horse is living, breathing proof that a pub can be for the local community as well as the cognoscenti.

My greatest words of praise for The Pack Horse are that it remains simply, beautifully, a pub – albeit one which just happens to do sensational food. It feeds and waters everyone who crosses its threshold, and it does so with generosity and warmth, with passion and a true sense of place.

Families? Cyclists? Muddy feet or muddy paws? Take a seat, have a drink, maybe peruse a menu. You're in a proper pub, and all is right with the world.

THE JOURNEY

Emma and I opened the doors to The Pack Horse on the 2nd of September 2016. What started off as a local pub serving traditional food developed over the years into a destination gastropub at the heart of its village community. In 2023, The Pack Horse was listed 18th in the UK's prestigious Top 50 Gastropubs, retained its place in The Michelin Guide and The Good Food Guide, and was awarded a coveted five out of five food score from Hardens Guide. I have always believed that The Pack Horse would be a special place, and its story is one that should be told. The following pages document my journey, from conflicted teenager and aspiring actor to self-taught chef and pub landlord at the age of 24.

Foundations

I find trying to pinpoint a true beginning to this story quite a challenge. Many chefs cite other chefs in the family or travelling the world as sources of their inspiration and success. On reflection, I believe the seeds of my kitchen creativity were sown in more humble beginnings.

I was born in Chatham, Kent on the 28th of July 1992. My parents, Liz and Keith, split up when I was two years old, which came with a certain set of challenges for a young only child to figure out. I saw Dad every other weekend, and Mum worked long hours for a filtration company all week, so I was left in the care of my grandparents, Priscilla and Des, for the majority of my childhood. They lived in the quaint Kentish town of Ditton, of which my nan was the local reverend. Grandad had suffered a brain tumour long before I was born and the resulting epilepsy had forced him into early retirement, which – true to his nature – he fully embraced. While Nanny still worked, Grandad and I spent most days together. He had a great love of the outdoors and the natural world, and when he wasn't watching David Attenborough on the television, he was lifting me up to the kitchen window to show me all the different birds in the garden. Next to the kitchen window was a little spice rack, and I remember asking Grandad what they were one day, probably around the age of five. He loved to fuel my curiosity and so, spice by spice, we had little tastes of everything. Most of them were deeply unpleasant, but perhaps that's where it all began for me.

Grandad was also a keen vegetable grower. I can still recall the smell of tomatoes in his greenhouse, the texture of the frosted glass under my fingers as I peered in during early summer, waiting for Grandad to give me a tour. Outside, marrows and runner beans were his speciality. I remember running out to the trellises with my carrier bag at the end of August, helping Grandad collect all the runner beans. They are still the largest I've ever seen, and Nanny has a cutting of the same runner bean plant growing in her garden to this day. I began to realise the runner bean harvest often coincided with the end of the school summer holidays, and I relished its arrival every year. It was Grandad and his garden that taught me the rhythm of nature and its ability to change, and I never forgot that despite the challenges that lay ahead.

Teenage Turmoil

Early teenage life had seemingly begun without a hitch; Mum and I moved to Ditton to be closer to Nanny and Grandad, and my relationship with Dad was unbreakably strong. The time we spent together on those sporadic weekends was filled with laughter and adventure, underpinned by important teachings of perspective and personal reflection. Mum and I were fortunate to holiday in some incredible locations with her partner, Gary, who had a love of Indian food which he fully instilled in me, culminating in a trip to India with him and Mum when I was 12. Realistically, it was probably all a little too much for me to tangibly take in at that age, but I know I enjoyed eating curry every day for two weeks. My own love of food had begun to develop, and for my 13th birthday I asked Mum for a chicken pie. However, the serenity I had grown used to from the routine of my slightly unorthodox upbringing was about to be thrown into chaos.

It began with my choice of secondary school. Dad had wanted me to look at schools in and around Maidstone, noting all the roots I had laid down locally and the fact that both boys' grammar schools in the town were of a high standard. Looking back, I believe my first choice would've been Maidstone Grammar School – its regimental order, proximity to home and challenging entry requirements all appealed to me. Mum and Nanny, though, were pushing for me to attend a very good Church of England School in Royal Tunbridge Wells. The facilities at the Bennett Memorial Diocesan School were excellent, and there were no exam entry requirements, but it was a 90-minute bus journey away and only two of my local friends were attending. Ultimately, for whatever reason, that school became my choice. Its distance from home meant that making solid friendships was a real challenge, and as time went on my Maidstone-based friends also slipped away from me. I felt isolated, in-between lives, stuck on a damp old bus for three hours a day, going to a school I didn't really want to attend with very limited friends.

And then, when I was 15, Mum moved away. She relocated to Huddersfield, predominantly for work and also to start a life with someone there. Nanny and Grandad sold their family home of some 40 years to move in with me down the road. Their home, full of childhood memories, the greenhouses, the chestnut trees, the veg patch, were all bulldozed by the local property developer. I was so sad that the house had gone forever, angry that Mum had seemingly left me, and confused that I couldn't live with Dad, which would've let Nanny and Grandad stay in their old house. It was a lot for a teenage mind to process, and I struggled to come to terms with it. After six months, I forced the issue and walked out, moving in with Dad. Grandad was beginning to slow down, his epilepsy slowly taking its toll on him. When Dad picked me up, Grandad came out the front door without saying a word and watched me drive away until the car was out of sight. I felt like he thought he had failed me, and the guilt of that feeling was etched in my mind for years.

I moved to Maidstone, the bus journey to school was shortened by 10 minutes, and I felt the most relaxed I had for a long time. Often over dinner in our small flat, Dad gently encouraged me to have the occasional glass of wine with dinner. We'd pick up different bottles from the supermarket every week and I developed a keen interest in it, which has now flourished into a full-blown passion. Internally, however, I was struggling. I blamed myself for a lot of what had happened and found solace in the school drama department. I was so comfortable being other people, and I excelled at it. Dad had been the drummer in a punk rock band named The Jerks in the 80s, and he believed the creative gene within me was finally coming out. My drama tutors, Steph and Ted, were incredible teachers: nurturing, understanding, caring, full of knowledge and energy in equal measure. I think they sensed my turmoil and did everything they could for me, including casting me in the school production of A Midsummer Night's Dream, which truly set me free. The demands of rehearsals and camaraderie between the cast lit a spark inside me, and I knew the stage was where I wanted to be. But in truth, I was most comfortable on stage because I was trying to run away from myself. In true teenage style, I didn't like being me, and it all unfolded at the end of the school year. Dad had always wanted me to be in the school football team – we both love football and still follow West Ham United to this day. Due to my own anxieties born out of the preceding events, I never tried out for the school team, but instead fabricated an entire season of results and games for Dad, because I thought it would make him proud. When he inevitably found out, he packed my bags and sent me back to Nanny and Grandad.

A year later, my time at Bennett came to an end. I collected my GCSE results, including an A* in drama, and subsequently transferred to Invicta Girls Grammar School in Maidstone. Yes, it was a girls' school. A handful of boys were let in for sixth form, which ended up almost being my undoing. Raging hormones directed me away from the classroom and towards chasing girls, and eventually I was caught outside of lessons one time too many and was on the brink of being expelled. The school spared me, though I still don't really know why – I had catastrophically failed my A level physics, didn't attend philosophy and ethics for a year, and was only really bothered about drama and English. This was an intensely results-focused school, and I knew how much of a thorn in their side I had become.

I distracted myself at home with regular visits from my oldest and dearest friend Rob, who had also been at Bennett. He was the first in our friendship group to get a car and therefore visited pretty much every weekend. Nanny and Grandad were always very accommodating, perhaps realising how much I needed him. It was pure escapism; all we did was play on the PlayStation and kick a football around. Rob was also into his food and drink as a young man, and whenever we had a free house we'd cook together, including a now infamous chilli con carne that we unwittingly prepared with a load of melted plastic in it. On another occasion, drunkenly making our way to bed after a night out, we raided Nanny's wine cupboard and drank some fine aged reds in my bedroom, paired with a mountain of crisps. It's safe to say I learnt my lesson the hard way with that experience, and the wine stash was never touched again.

Even little moments like Rob and I preparing instant noodles together still stick in my mind. Drawing on Grandad's teachings from the spice rack all those years ago, I'd always have a go at improving on the starting point. Those kinds of food references began to drip into my life more without me even realising; I had a reputation at school for eating either a curry or a pie every night, and most days I'd order a keema naan from the local Indian restaurant I walked past on the way home. In the early days of Facebook, friends would wait online for my daily food update: how many naans did I get today, was it curry or pie for dinner? Katie was one friend who picked up on this more than others and we had a long-running joke about my curry obsession, but one night we had a deep-rooted conversation about food which enabled me to express myself in a way I never had before. I began to realise that there was a connection between food and my positive experiences. From casual meals out to family Christmas dinners, or Sunday roasts with Dad, every association was positive, and that was something entirely new to me. Katie had always sensed my quirks and, unbeknownst to both of us at the time, she set my creativity free and allowed me to be comfortable with who I am for the first time in my life.

Changing Direction

I scraped through my A levels and got accepted to Brunel University London – studying drama, of course – where I grew up, almost immediately. It was like a weight had been lifted from my shoulders and suddenly I had the independence of a young man figuring the world out. I was blessed with an excellent group of flatmates, all of whom shared a maturity beyond their years. In our first year we had a communal kitchen cupboard for household staples, and I cooked every night. My drama course was fine, if not as intense or deep as I had expected, though perhaps I had already realised I didn't have such a need to be 'in role' all the time. Sharing a house in second year was pivotal for me. My housemate Sam and I were both keen home cooks by this point and we had decided to share our food budgets, looking for discounts and generally needing to get creative to feed ourselves. At the same time, Channel 4 was airing its River Cottage Veg series, in which Hugh Fearnley-Whittingstall goes vegetarian for six months of the year and is challenged to feed himself as well as he would've had he been eating meat. Sam and I were gripped: we decided to follow Hugh and go vegetarian ourselves along with the program. It was an immense challenge having to swap chicken for beans and pulses, but it suddenly got me thinking about food and flavour in a totally different way.

I proceeded to purchase my first ever cookbook, River Cottage Everyday, and found myself more excited by what Sam and I could come up with for dinner than being in a rehearsal room. Not every meal was a success – we learnt the hard way that mayonnaise is a terrible ingredient for taking the heat out of a curry. We rewarded ourselves at the end of the experiment with a Christmas meal for the house, a whole roast duck. It was a logistical challenge given the limitations of a student kitchen, but to this day it may be one of the best roasts of my life. In using the knowledge we had gained over the last few months, we realised we had turned into competent home cooks, and the positive affirmations surrounding cooking and food for me only grew stronger. At the same time, my love for the stage was wavering. A combination of audition setbacks and the environment created by the attitudes of some colleagues left me deflated, and I had already started to lean more into directorial roles towards the end of my second year. I found myself no longer studying the great actors of my generation, instead studying great chefs. My cookbook collection began to grow. Food had become all-consuming, and I knew what I had to do.

My third year of university came around quickly, and by this point I was waking my housemates up to the smell of freshly baked bread or a stew that had been simmering away all night. I started a food blog, documenting my recipes with a focus on education and thrifty food (it's still out there on the internet somewhere). My drama degree had become a chore, but I was determined to see it out for fear of a wasted three years. Alongside directing my dissertation performance group, I was busy applying for kitchen jobs up and down the country. I graduated from Brunel with a first class honours degree in Drama, but still no firm job offer. I was getting desperate, and nobody was responding to my applications. Without a cooking qualification, I was quickly being put at the bottom of the pile.

Passion and determination alone seemingly weren't enough, and a sinking feeling developed which reminded me too much of the many audition setbacks. I kept practising my cookery techniques at home, thumbing through my cookbooks, spending whatever money I had left on ingredients to practice with, and attempting to hone my skills. I moved back in with Dad after graduating, but something wasn't right at home. Dad was struggling after a difficult period in his personal life, and it made our relationship incredibly strained. I had no choice but to move to Huddersfield and live with Mum while Dad got the help he needed. It was a situation I never foresaw, and to make matters worse, as soon as I left Maidstone I got a job offer in a kitchen which I could no longer accept.

First Steps

Luckily, Mum had always been very work-sharp and she helped me hunt for kitchen jobs near her in Huddersfield. Finally, I had an offer. It was pot-washing for a pub called The Sovereign Inn, Shepley, which is part of a pub chain group owned and operated by Mitchells & Butlers. I donned my suit and drove to the pub ready for my interview. Rob Dalton, the kitchen manager, greeted me and exclaimed that he'd never seen anyone arrive for a kitchen job in a suit and tie before. I was offered a trial shift that evening for a special themed night, during which I would wash up and serve the bread course. Finally, my first taste of a busy kitchen service had come. It was a hectic blur, and I don't think the dishes were washed up very well, but I was buzzing. At the end of the shift, I was offered a part-time job washing up three days a week, and I was delighted. I knew there would be a long road ahead, but I also knew that all the great chefs had started out on dishwashing duties, so perhaps I could emulate them. On my second shift, I was introduced to sous chef Craig, whose first words to me were "Why the f*** do you want to be a chef?". Craig had worked for these behemoth chains all his life, and it had clearly influenced him. However, I soon learnt that he was excellent at pushing out vast quantities of food to standard, and deep down he still had that same passion that I had.

The food at The Sovereign was, for lack of a better word, awful. Big chain groups like this have most of their food delivered pre-prepared and frozen, so 'cooking' in these kitchens is a very loose term… defrost and assembly would be more accurate. Despite being dreadfully slow on pots, I was allowed to help with the starters at weekends by shadowing Bob, who ran the starter section. Bob became a great friend who taught me the importance of organisation and how to manage a section properly. We had a good time together in the kitchen, developing a symbiosis when on section together, each of us totally aware of the other and of what we were doing. It was an incredible feeling that reminded me of being on stage, nailing a scene with someone. The thrill was addictive and I kept on working hard, getting my head down and focusing on the future, practicing at home in the meantime. Bob and I would also cook together on our days off, setting a £10 shopping budget and then preparing two meals for each other. Bob was organised and much tidier than me, but I understood flavour and remembered all the recipes I had learnt like a script to back me up. I knew that as soon as I had Bob's skills, I'd be one step closer to cooking on the main section.

Everything seemed to be progressing ideally and I was saving money while living with Mum to put towards my future. Out of the blue though, everything changed. Returning home from my first ever staff day out, slightly drunk but not rowdy, Bob and I had an old school sleepover in my room. Bob left early for work and when I woke up a little later, Mum greeted me concerningly, and told me I had to leave the house before her partner got home. I couldn't believe it, and suddenly found myself homeless. Mum's partner at the time is not worth talking about, but knowing his character and Mum's reaction, I had no choice but to leave. So, I drove to The Sovereign and spoke to my boss Rob about the situation, who very kindly offered me a room at his house. It is worth noting that Rob was mid-divorce at this point, still living with his wife and two young kids, and yet he still found room for me. I will forever be grateful for his kindness and generosity. Once we became proper housemates, our friendship outside of the kitchen flourished, and every week we would take turns cooking something more extravagant for each other, keeping score on a blackboard in the kitchen. It gave me the opportunity to try out recipes I never would have before and pushed my creativity further, with a qualified chef at the other end of the spoon critiquing and guiding my choices. It was invaluable, and paired with the logistical skills I was gaining from working in such a high-volume kitchen, I was soon ready for the company to loan me out to one of their struggling sites to manage the kitchen.

The Golden Ball in Sheffield became my first head chef job. The kitchen was in total disarray, like a scene from Kitchen Nightmares. Poor quality and poor standards were the name of the game, and one lunch service while watching a chef rinse raw fish under a handwash tap with a dirty ice cream scoop underneath, it was enough for me to close the kitchen immediately and reset. This was my first chance to get people working the way I wanted, and after a lengthy meeting in the bin yard over a few cigarettes, the kitchen team knuckled down over the following weeks and we transformed the standards. The workload was immense. I was working seven days a week, 9am until midnight on top of a 40-minute commute. After finishing up at 1am on a busy Saturday, I set off home as usual, in a rush for my bed. It had been raining, and the unlit country roads were more treacherous than I anticipated. Before I had time to register what had happened, my car was rolling through a drystone wall and down a farmer's field, finally coming to a stop with my windscreen wedged against a tree.

The fire brigade winched the car and cut me out, and although I was sat on a spinal board in hospital overnight, miraculously, there wasn't a mark on me. I had no time to process what had happened though, as I could no longer do my job in Sheffield without a car to get there. I was straight back to work on Tuesday in another local pub under the same brand, but by the Friday when I had sorted a new car, the opportunity at The Golden Ball had gone. At the same time, Grandad's health deteriorated rapidly. His epilepsy delivered a final crushing blow and left him bedridden, unable to move or speak at the age of 72. I was absorbed by work and hadn't seen him for a while, but I'm so glad I was able to drive to Kent in time to see him before he died. In the space of two weeks, I had gone from nearly killing myself to losing my first mentor, the man who had influenced and shaped the very fabric of who I had become. I was numb and lost in my own head for a very long time.

A phone call from my old boss, Rob, pulled me out of the slump. He had taken on The Admiral Rodney – another high volume, ping-and-sling chain pub in Sheffield – and needed a head chef. Naturally I said yes immediately, lured by the chance of working alongside Rob again in what was then one of Vintage Inn's flagship sites. All was not as it seemed though, as the previous head chef of some 20 years was in fact still working there, only now part-time. I will say that he was good to me, gifting me with all his knowledge and experience, but it became an impossible task to win over the kitchen team as a 23-year-old head chef with their veteran ex-boss still rattling around. I had an unexpected ally front of house though, and that was Emma. Emma and I met on my first shift, and there was most certainly a spark between us. As is often the way within hospitality, we didn't hang around and I was at her house that very same evening. She had been a manager for a similarly aligned juggernaut pub company, vastly experienced but just working part-time at The Rodney to supplement her nannying work, which she had chosen over front line pub managing. Our relationship blossomed quickly, and Emma saw the passion and ambition in my nature as well as just how much being a chef meant to me.

However, I had grossly underestimated just how busy The Rodney would be. We were churning out some 300 roast dinners every Sunday between four chefs, and the sheer scale of this boil-in-the-bag operation truly took its toll on me. I wanted out: my passion for what I loved had been eroded by the job, and it was so full-on that I had completely stopped cooking at home as well. I wanted to walk away from it all, totally disillusioned with the part of the industry I found myself stuck in, and so I applied for a managerial job with Aldi. Sam, my university housemate, came to visit and he was devastated to hear that I was looking for a way out after putting so much into the process of becoming a chef already. We took a drive and stopped for lunch in Castleton in the Peak District. "Wouldn't you like to run a place like this?" he said to me at the table. Though I didn't know it at the time, that comment planted a very significant seed in my mind.

The Pack Horse

I got through the first round of interviews with Aldi and had a face-to-face meeting lined up down in Swindon. Tensions were growing at home between me and Emma, born out of our working life frustrations, and things bubbled over one morning during my attempt to help her put away some washing, at which point I picked up my car keys and went for a drive. I had no destination planned, just me and the open road. Castleton came and went, and I carried on through the rolling hills of the Peak District until, for some unknown reason, I decided to turn off at a little village called Hayfield. On first impressions, it was the most wonderfully quaint and quintessential country village, all set in Derbyshire stone with a local shop, post office and pub: it was magical.

As I carried on through the main road past the church and over the bridge, I saw another pub coming up, but this one had a large sign on the front which read "Do you want to run this pub?". The Pack Horse looked quite unassuming, a beautiful old building with a large black sign on the front advertising functions. The voice in my head was already convincing me that I did want to run this pub, in this wonderful little village. I rushed home in a much better mood than the one I had left in, and Emma thought I had completely lost the plot. In a matter of hours, I had gone from wanting to walk away from the industry to wanting to run my own pub. I asked Emma if she would want to run it with me. Reluctant at first, she decided to accompany me back to The Pack Horse for dinner a few days later, and I never attended my follow-up interview with Aldi.

We saw the potential of the place immediately, and Emma was all in. This was our opportunity to open our own proper local pub and live the good life. She arranged a meeting with Enterprise Inns, the building owners, and got the ball rolling. Johnny was the regional manager at the time, responsible for the general operation of the pubs in Enterprise's northwest portfolio. He saw our passion and vision immediately, and was fully on board with our plan for a local pub serving proper food made with fresh produce. The original plan contained a menu which was basically all pub classics: burgers, pies, fish and chips. It was all I knew but I was passionate about replicating that formula with quality ingredients rather than defrosting meals in a microwave. Just three weeks after seeing the pub for the first time, Johnny turned to us and said we would have the keys in eight weeks. The turnaround was staggering, and we had a lot of work to do. Business plans were furiously written, beer and wine ranges carefully chosen from the catalogue available to us, and I was driving out into the Peak District to meet suppliers on every day off. I remember meeting our butcher John for the first time and seeing the passion he had for his job; it all just felt so right. He was thrilled to learn that The Pack Horse was being taken over by a chef, and we maintain a very close working relationship to this day.

Opening the Doors

Everything was falling into place nicely and we were packed and ready to move into The Pack Horse on the 29th of August 2016. My mum was coming over to help sort the place out, as well as Emma's mum from Scotland and her sister Julie. We had to be open on Friday the 2nd of September and needed to do a full deep clean and redecoration first, plus receive all the stock, get the kitchen prepped and generally have the place looking fit for purpose. As we pulled into the car park, Johnny was waiting for us with bad news. The gas certificates hadn't been validated in time, and we couldn't move in until the following day. With the clock already ticking, we had no choice but to book ourselves into the Royal Hotel just down the road and hope that we wouldn't lose too much time.

The following day, the big clean up began. Mum and I tackled the kitchen, while Emma and her mum focused on the pub itself. Steam-cleaning years of grease off the kitchen extraction took an entire day, and I refused to begin prepping any food until it was spotless. The kitchen had a few appliances already: a little six ring hob and oven, a fryer, and a microwave. It was enough to start with, especially as it was predominantly me in the kitchen along with Ollie, a passionate home cook but only available at weekends and soon off to university. We had met our inherited team a few days earlier and explained our vision for the pub to them, how different it would be from before. We were thrilled that everyone decided to stay, which at least provided some initial stability in what would be a chaotic few months.

Opening night went like a dream, and we met many locals who we still see every week. The food was received much better than I initially thought and as Sunday approached, I was left with a heavily diminished stock of ingredients. I didn't plan on running a Sunday roast on my first week as I wanted to find my feet with everything else, but my hand was forced into doing it anyway. The gas oven was not equipped for any kind of large volume cooking, so I decided to slow roast a lamb shoulder early in the morning to then free up the oven for roast potatoes. I had, however, completely failed to think about Yorkshire puddings. Having only ever dealt with frozen yorkies while working for M&B, my own recipe wasn't up to scratch and I only had one Yorkshire pudding tin, so I decided to run the roast without them. The day seemed to go pretty well, with some good feedback on what was a bit of a rushed project. When I got upstairs that evening, I made the mistake of looking at TripAdvisor, where someone had left a one-star review mostly because of the missing Yorkshire puddings. To receive that from someone on our opening weekend was devastating, and I struggled to come to terms with it for a while. My relationship with TripAdvisor and the people who so willingly leave negative reviews after dining with us – despite having the opportunity for us to fix things if they mention issues while they are here – remains strained. I have learnt to ignore it, but I always look back on that first negative review and think how ignorant it was of the circumstances, and totally unnecessary to be like that on the opening weekend of a new business.

Developing an Identity

We had remained fairly busy from the get-go, and the food menu was solid despite being full of pub classics. Eventually I got more comfortable with my new suppliers and my kitchen equipment, and some more seasonal, experimental dishes began to appear on our menu. One of these was a pork loin wellington, and our regulars would come in to sample the latest iteration every time I told them I had a new refined version ready. Our guests wanted to be part of the journey as well, and I was delighted that our take on a classic was being well received. Our first Christmas period was a huge success – Bob came to visit and share the stoves with me one last time, and we had a great throwback service together.

Mother's Day was now fast approaching, a huge day in the calendar for pubs and one of the busiest of the year. At the same time, my imagination was running wild with new dish ideas as I absorbed even more cookbooks and worked with suppliers to get more seasonal produce in. Outside of the classics, the menu was changing more regularly, but guests were still reluctant to divert from the usual pub options. For some completely bonkers reason, I decided to go all out with my Mother's Day menu, convinced I could pull off the finer details of every dish and elevate them above anything we had done previously for a 120-cover service. I was wrong. Not only had I massively under-ordered on a lot of items, I could barely keep pace with the day. 1.30pm came, and the beef was already running out. 2pm, no more roast lamb. I had 60 covers still to come in and no roast dinners left on Mother's Day. I was so embarrassed, frantically rewriting the menu every half an hour in an attempt to stretch whatever produce I had left. One of our bar men ran to the shops and returned with a piddly little beef joint that lasted another 20 minutes. With barely any food left for our final tables, who had sat down an hour late as it was taking me so long to get the food out, all I wanted to do was burst into tears. Emma managed the situation like an absolute professional. She is always so good with the guests and drew on all her experience to somehow manage people's expectations in dire circumstances on a premium day. She never got angry with me about it, but we had a very frank conversation at the end of the day over many bottles of wine.

I tried my best to forget that service and move on from what I had done, but our first May Day Bank Holiday would bring me close to reliving it. I was still working solo in the kitchen all the time, opening six days a week and working from 9am until the pub closed. It was brutal, and that first bank holiday weekend was both intensely busy and very warm. Professional kitchens tend to have two temperatures throughout the year: bitterly cold in winter and unbearably hot in summer. This bank holiday Monday was the latter and the heat had been relentless all weekend. We were fully booked and about an hour before the last table arrived, I collapsed in the kitchen and crawled outside, unable to breathe. I couldn't get anyone's attention, there were still things cooking, but eventually Emma found me outside and closed the pub. I felt like I had let everyone down again, and I realised that if things didn't change, the stress and physical demands of the pub would end up killing me pretty quickly.

We expanded the kitchen team and reduced our hours a little, closing on Tuesdays as well as Mondays. It was around this time that Thom Hetherington first came to visit. We were aware of Thom and his influence within the northwest hospitality scene, so it was quite unnerving knowing he was dining with us. But his feedback proved invaluable. Not only did he love his Sunday lunch and the fact that we were still a proper pub, he told us that we should commit to our style and not let anything distract us from what we were good at. This was game-changing, as now I had the time to consider the more experimental dishes while the rest of the kitchen team got the job done. Yet still the burgers would outsell everything else three to one. I knew where my heart lay though, and I knew we would never become a seasonally led food destination without something changing.

So, overnight, with Thom's words ringing in my ears, I removed all the pub classics from the menu and replaced them with seasonal plates of local produce. Thom also shouted about us on social media, and our following began to grow to a wider audience, including those within the industry who had started to pay attention. I think we would be three years behind where we are now without Thom, and Emma and I will always be eternally grateful for his support. Members of the kitchen team came and went, but my vision was now fixed. This was a proper local pub for local people that also just happened to serve great food. We still did a quiz night every Wednesday, we still did Sunday roasts, we still did pork scratchings and pints of bitter. The Pack Horse was becoming a truly special place thanks to that balance between welcoming local pub and top quality food.

Covid

Two good years of stability set us up for what I thought would be a huge 2020. I thought if we pushed on throughout the year and kept the standards up, refined our techniques and kept shouting loud and proud on social media, we would finally break into the Top 50 Gastropubs. 2020, of course, had other ideas. Whisperings of Covid-19 and the devastation it was causing in China and Europe were reaching the bar, and there was an edge of unease every day in the build up to mid-March. Emma and I kept a very close eye on what was coming, and we cleverly planned ahead for any kind of situation by keeping our stock levels low and trying to be as reactive as possible. What we hadn't planned for was the government telling people to avoid going to pubs from the 16th of March.

Suddenly we were stuck in limbo, with bills and staff to pay but no punters in. We did what we could, discouraging anyone from standing at the bar and splitting our tables up as much as possible. Our wonderful Hayfield regulars did the best they could, but most people were terrified. It was a grim week, and I made the decision to stop serving food on the Thursday as it was all going straight in the bin. Emma and I were watching the announcement live behind the bar on Friday the 20th of March, when all pubs and restaurants were told to close. Emma burst into tears, and I was just in complete shock. What on earth was going to happen to us now? How would we get through this and still have something of a business left at the end of it? We knew that some pubs would stay open until the bitter end, but none of it felt right to us and we sombrely told everyone to drink up and leave there and then, not knowing if we'd ever see them in The Pack Horse again.

Everything that made this pub special – the people – had been taken away. We attempted takeaway meals, but it didn't really fit with the style of food we were serving so that was shelved. We shifted focus onto 'cook at home' meal boxes, which were great fun to put together but cost an absolute fortune to make. Given that money was already impossibly tight, we were restricted to doing these on Sundays and premium days only, as it just wasn't worthwhile given our catchment area. It kept us busy though, and stayed the madness despite the huge mental toll that lockdown took on both of us.

Revival

Finally, there was a light at the end of the tunnel – with Covid restrictions being eased, we could reopen in July 2020. All my focus and energy went into producing the best menu we'd ever done, and I knew the team were desperate to get back to work too. Everyone was buzzing despite the weird atmosphere; it was amazing what four months of no socialising had done to us all. The pub was divided up to help social distancing, all our one-way stickers were in place, and we finally reopened the doors to huge fanfare. We were overwhelmed by how much people had missed us. Thom was back within the first week, and with one big push on social media from him, as well as some chatter about our shin beef and pickled walnut pie in a beef fat crust, we had attracted the attention of reviewers from Manchester Confidential. This was our first major review, so the pressure was on. But in truth we knew we just had to treat them like everyone else, so we did, and the review was fantastic. That opened the doors for others to visit us eventually… once we had all sat through a second lockdown of box assembling. Our New Year's Eve tasting menu in a box was actually great fun for all involved, and the sporadic nature of it kept me busy but also allowed my mind the time to really focus on the next iteration of our menu, ready for the second reopening.

In June 2021, Emma and I shared another milestone with the birth of our wonderful son Elliot. This only fuelled the fire inside me to fully realise our vision for The Pack Horse; I now had no choice but to make a success of this, as Elliot's future depended entirely on my ability to cook. As we pushed forward, the press followed. First it was Chris Pople, who visited soon after our post-lockdown reopening. We were blown away by his kind words, which also helped me to realise that I wasn't just an imposter and what we were doing was tangibly very good. Then we received a tip off that the feared and revered Marina O'Loughlin was coming to dine with us. Panic set in initially; Marina had a fierce reputation and was famously not particularly keen on pubs, but we knew there must have been a reason she was coming to us. I began to relax a bit; people were talking about us in a good way across the industry, and it was Autumn, my best menu of the year.

The night of her visit, Hayfield was on form. The bar was rammed, all enjoying an evening in the pub like old times, blissfully unaware of the drama unfolding for us as we waited nervously for Marina's plates to be cleared. Empty, a relief. Perhaps she even enjoyed it? I was convinced she would find something, though. But when Marina's Sunday Times review was published, it was utterly glowing. I had never felt so humbled in my life, and I knew how much of an impact this would have on us. The phone didn't stop ringing, and the website crashed. We were fully booked every day for lunch and dinner throughout November and then all the way through to March. I had never seen anything like it, and those months basically saved us from the Covid debt.

That winter, we finally broke into the Top 50 Gastropubs, placing 32nd in our first year on the list. Weeks later, an email from The Michelin Guide announced our inclusion in their 2022 guide. I thought it was fake – surely Michelin hadn't come to our humble little Peak District pub? But it was real, and there we were on the Michelin Guide website. It felt like a weight had been lifted, despite always saying we cook for guests, not for the guide. I felt validated, like every single moment of my life had finally had a purpose, and I had achieved my ultimate goal. There was, however, a negative effect of all the publicity, good news and accolades too. We were so intensely busy in the kitchen that the pressure took its toll on everyone. By May 2022, I was on my own again. Notice after notice was handed to me, unable to deal with the workload or looking for a different challenge. I was back to square one, but now I had a reputation to uphold. I stripped the menu back and had to limit bookings, learning from the mistakes I had made many times before.

It was like waiting for a storm to pass, which it did in the most unlikely of ways. Luke, the head chef at The Blind Bull in Little Hucklow just down the road from us, had come to The Pack Horse for dinner one night with his friend Paul, a chef from London. He had a lovely evening and came running back in with his phone number in case I ever needed his help. I did, immediately, and what started out as a part-time helping hand led to Paul becoming our executive chef, taking the daily pressure of kitchen life off my shoulders for the first time ever, enabling me to focus on the food and building the pub's presence nationally. Paul was quickly joined by Pedro, whom he had worked with previously; after a phone call, a meal here that he loved, and meeting for a coffee, Pedro became our sous chef.

How quickly we went from potential turmoil to the magnificent team we three became – me, Paul, and Pedro – is staggering. With their combined work ethic and breadth of knowledge, the food continues to go from strength to strength and in early 2023 we reached 18th place in the Top 50 Gastropubs. A five out of five rating for food from Hardens followed, as well as retaining our place in The Michelin Guide. So, on we go. What next? Hopefully, another site to keep our expanding, talented team under our own roof. Boutique rooms in Hayfield, perhaps, with a breakfast offering at The Pack Horse? The journey most certainly isn't over. We will always continue to be a proper pub for everyone. A proper pub that just happens to serve some damn tasty food. A proper pub with pints and dog treats, and seats at the bar, and newspapers, and a weekly quiz, and our extraordinary locals and regulars. Thank you all for being part of the journey, and I hope you continue to join me on it.

A NOTE ON THE RECIPES

The recipes in this book are laid out seasonally, and within those chapters the dishes are split between starters and smaller plates, mains and feasts, and desserts. They are a mixture of dishes we serve throughout the year at the pub, alongside my favourite home recipes for something a little less challenging but equally delicious.

Wherever possible I have tried to limit the use of professional gadgets, but I would recommend the following equipment for every kitchen:

Cook's blowtorch. A powerful tool for caramelising and colouring food quickly, giving a subtle barbecued flavour.

Meat thermometer. A good kitchen probe thermometer will transform the food that you eat, as you can directly monitor internal temperatures when cooking meat or fish and stop or continue cooking as required. It is absolutely critical for the quality of your food that both meat and fish are rested after cooking for at least half their cooking time. This relaxes the protein, retaining moisture and flavour, and the core temperature will also continue to rise when out of the oven. For larger joints with much longer cooking and resting times, a loose covering of tin foil will keep the meat warm enough. Below is a table of my recommended internal cooking temperatures.

	Rare	Medium	Well Done
Beef	42°c	52°c	70°c
Lamb	46°c	54°c	70°c
Pork	-	63°c	71°c
Chicken	-	-	72°c
Boneless Fish	-	46°c	60°c
Fish on the Bone	-	50°c	64°c

Stand mixer. Stand mixers free up time more than anything else. Good stand mixers come with several attachments such as whisks and dough hooks, enabling you to whip cream or knead dough while also doing something else. Very useful, time saving, and energy saving for your arms!

Food processor. A simple but good quality food processor enables you to prep faster and with ease. The speed of the blades makes emulsion and dressing making a breeze, often reducing the time by more than half.

Finally, please be aware that all oven temperatures listed in the recipes are for a fan-assisted convection oven. Please adjust temperatures accordingly depending on your own oven and get to know your oven well – its hot spots and how it behaves at certain temperatures – for best results.

Spring

Spring is a welcome relief from an isolating Peak District winter. The emergence of daffodils heralds the beginning of change, a warm-up act for Spring's true beauty. The bitterness of winter air quickly becomes a distant memory as we feel the sun's warm embrace for the first time in what feels like an eternity. Fresh grass, fuelled by the sun and nourished by April showers – as inevitable as the seasons themselves – brings a lushness to the hills, washing away winter's weariness and bleak grey hues.

Further into the season, accents of white and pink permeate the green shoots among the treetops as blossoms bloom, and the effervescent chatter of birdsong returns. The energetic youth of new life frolics in the fields; the bleating of hundreds of lambs carried through the village on a mild breeze is an aural sensation unlike any other, evoking innocence and playfulness. It feels as if the world around us is doing this for the first time all over again.

These feelings and emotions are mirrored in the kitchen. Tired of heavy sauces and spending our afternoons breaking down brutish root vegetables, the emergence of blankets of wild garlic tells us it's finally time to lighten up. Green asparagus shoots put a full stop on any lingering doubt that winter is still upon us, and the menu shifts into a fresher, less robust offer to reflect the world around us. But do not get lured into the false dawn of an early summer; St George's mushrooms remind us of the enthusiasm-curbing spring rains and provide an earthiness to match the mood. It is of course the rains which bring these little mouthfuls of petrichor to our tables, so perhaps we should be a little more thankful for them, and allow Spring to balance itself out, like a great concerto.

When daffodils begin to peer,
With heigh! the doxy, over the dale,
Why, then comes in the sweet o' the year;
For the red blood reigns in the winter's pale.
The white sheet bleaching on the hedge,
With heigh! the sweet birds, O, how they sing!
Doth set my pugging tooth on edge;
For a quart of ale is a dish for a king.

From The Winter's Tale, William Shakespeare

OUR SEASONAL HIGHLIGHTS

MARCH	APRIL	MAY
Wild garlic	Nettles	Sorrel
Watercress	Asparagus	Jersey Royals
Spring onions	Garden rhubarb	Spring greens
Purple sprouting broccoli	St George's mushrooms	Morel mushrooms

Bowden Bridge & Hill Houses

2 MILES, EASY, ALLOW 1–1½ HOURS.

One short climb. Can be muddy in places after rain.

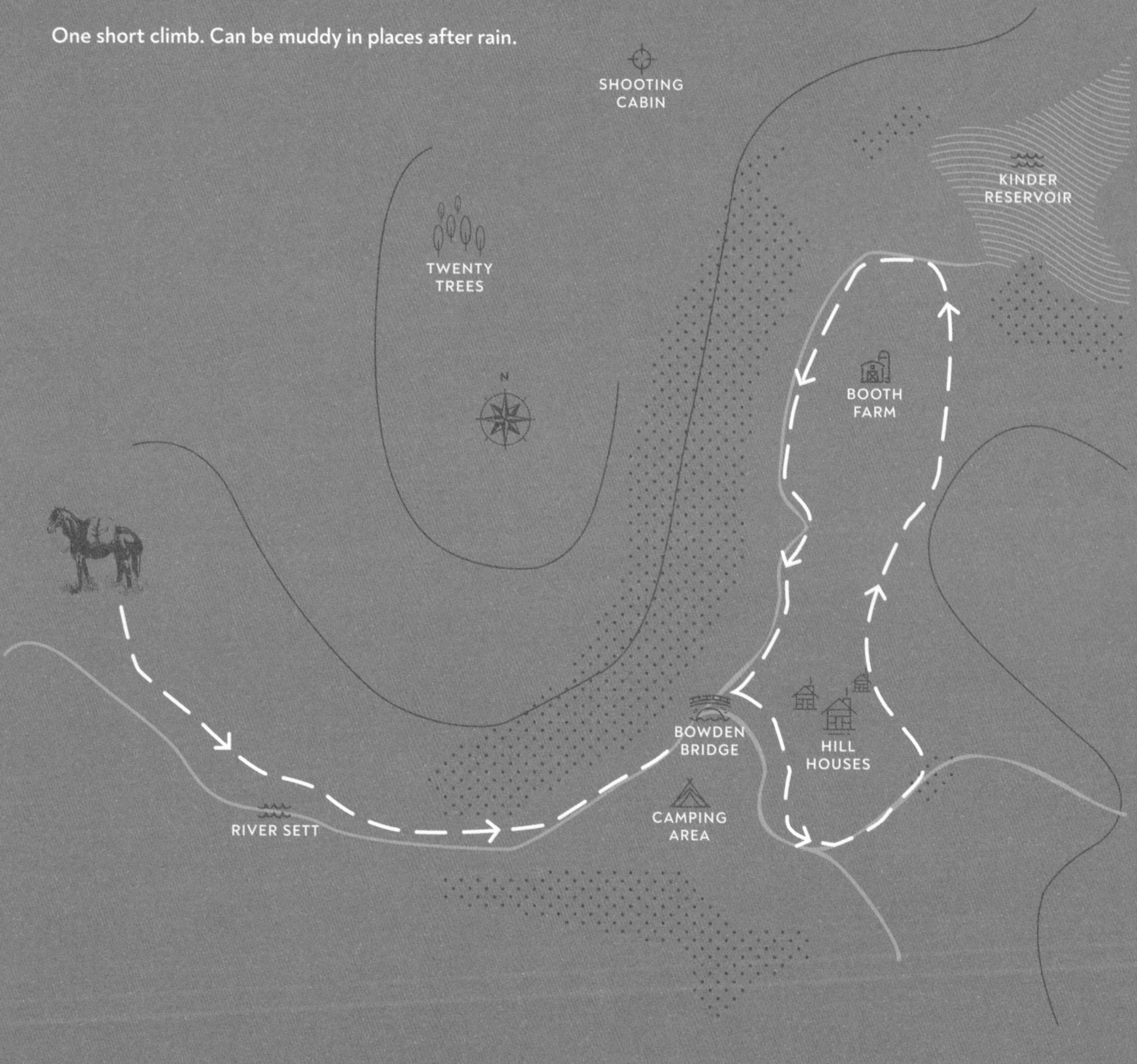

- SHOOTING CABIN
- KINDER RESERVOIR
- TWENTY TREES
- BOOTH FARM
- RIVER SETT
- BOWDEN BRIDGE
- CAMPING AREA
- HILL HOUSES

My favourite springtime walk is comparatively easy for Peak District walks and gives stunning views of Kinder Scout and Mount Famine, as well as passing through several farms which, when timed correctly, are bustling with young lambs and occasionally cows and their calves. A notable point of interest along this route is the old sheepwash which, although now disused, used to be a central hub of activity for local farmers in the early 20th century; the communal sheepwashing was a key date on the calendar of our rural village life.

From the front door of The Pack Horse, turn left. Bear right over the River Sett and keep left of the church up the main road, Church Street, passing The George Hotel and the fish and chip shop. At the top of Church Street, turn left and then left again into Valley Road.

Follow Valley Road, keeping left and following the river, but not crossing it. After a row of terraced houses on the right, the path descends to a no-through road. Keep left again at the fork bearing the owl carving, keeping the high stone retaining wall on your right. Descend to the river and after the last houses follow the riverside path, ignoring a footbridge. Keep left at the fork to walk between the river and the campsite, then turn left over the road bridge at the campsite entrance.

Turn right past Bowden Bridge car park. When the road bends slightly left at Bowden Bridge Cottage, turn right onto the riverside track. At the entrance to Oakbank, turn right over the packhorse bridge. In the corner beyond, turn left through a gate. Climb a walled path and go through a gate and past a converted barn to emerge at Hill Houses. Turn left past the farmhouse on your left and go through a gate.

Follow the track beyond, bending left and then right to reach Booth Farm after half a mile. Beyond Booth, descend to a lane, turn left and descend to the bridge by the restored sheepwash. Cross the river and turn left. Follow the road for half a mile to return to Bowden Bridge car park and continue straight, following Kinder Road all the way past The Sportsman pub. Descend back into village, staying on Kinder Road until you emerge back at The Pack Horse.

WILD GARLIC SOUP

SERVES 8

Ah, those early spring mornings in the forest, what joy they bring. You smell it before you see it: slender leaves of bright green wild garlic. This delicious edible wild plant, in season from late February to April, appears on our menu every year. The intense smell makes it impossible to mistake for anything else. When foraging, ensure you only take the largest leaves and never a whole plant.

100g unsalted butter

10ml vegetable oil

1 large onion, chopped

2 sprigs of thyme

1 bay leaf

4 large potatoes, preferably Roosters or Maris Piper, peeled and diced

1.5 litres vegetable stock

200ml double cream

300g wild garlic leaves, washed

Sea salt

Melt the butter with the oil in a large saucepan over a medium heat. Add the onion, thyme and bay to cook until soft.

Add the potatoes to the pan along with the vegetable stock, bring to the boil and then reduce to a simmer. Cook until the potatoes are soft and yielding.

Pour in the cream and bring to the boil. Add the wild garlic to the pan and stir in for around 2 minutes, allowing it to wilt without losing its vibrant green colour.

Blitz the soup until smooth, pass it through a fine sieve to ensure a silky texture, then serve topped with a little extra cream and some chiffonade of wild garlic leaf, with warm bread on the side.

CHICKEN & WILD GARLIC DUMPLINGS, CHICKEN & WILD GARLIC BROTH

SERVES 6

There's no denying that wild garlic becomes something of a hero ingredient for us across early spring, and it's important for us to use as much of the plant as possible through pickling and preserving. This dish – soft doughy dumplings in a light yet flavoursome broth – utilises both fresh, fermented, and pickled wild garlic in different forms: a true showcase of this seasonal ingredient and its versatility.

For the fermented wild garlic

200g wild garlic leaves

15g sea salt

1 tsp sugar

For the pickled wild garlic

30 wild garlic buds

300ml pickling liquor (see page 249)

For the broth

1 whole free-range chicken

1 bulb of garlic, split in half

3 sprigs of thyme

2 sprigs of rosemary

3 litres chicken stock

1 bunch of curly parsley, chopped

1 bunch of chervil, chopped

For the dumplings

1 shallot, finely chopped

200g self-raising flour

100g suet

10g salt

⅛ tsp baking powder

1 lemon, zested

A handful of wild garlic, finely chopped

For the fermented wild garlic

Gather your wild garlic 4 days before serving this dish. Wash the wild garlic leaves and pat them dry with a clean towel, removing any tough stems, then roughly chop. Put them in a bowl with the salt and sugar, mix until evenly distributed, allowing the water to be drawn out from the wild garlic leaves, then transfer to a sterilised jar. Press the mixture down so that the liquid covers the leaves. Cover the jar with a cheesecloth or a lid with an airlock and let it ferment at room temperature for 3-4 days, or until it smells sour and tangy. Once the mixture has fermented, transfer it to the refrigerator to slow down the fermentation process.

For the pickled wild garlic

Place the buds into a container with the pickling liquor and leave in the fridge overnight.

For the broth

Place the chicken, garlic, thyme, rosemary, and stock in a large pan and bring to the boil, then reduce the heat and simmer for 2 hours, using a ladle to skim the impurities from the top of the stock every 15 minutes. Strain the liquid and discard the aromatics, keeping the chicken to one side. Once cool enough to handle, pick the meat from the chicken and refrigerate until needed. When your dumplings are ready, place the stock back on a high heat and reduce by half, then season to taste.

For the dumplings

Sweat the shallot in a little oil until soft, then allow to cool completely. In a mixing bowl, rub the flour, suet, salt, and baking powder together until well mixed, then add the lemon zest, wild garlic and 180g of the cooked chicken meat. Mix well, then gradually add around 90ml of water to bind everything into a soft, pliable dough (you may need a little more water). Knead the dough well, dusting it with a little flour if the dough is too sticky. Let the dough rest for at least 45 minutes. Mould the rested dough into dumplings and then rest again for 15 minutes before placing into a colander. Cover this with cling film and prick a few holes in the film with a fork, then set the colander over the pan of reducing chicken stock. Steam the dumplings for 15 minutes, then remove and place in your serving bowls. Finish the broth with the chopped parsley and chervil, pickled wild garlic buds, and fermented wild garlic leaves. Simmer for 1 minute and then pour the broth over the dumplings to serve.

CRAB, WATERCRESS VICHYSSOISE, PICKLED WHITE ASPARAGUS

SERVES 6

There is little in this world that comes close to the sweet, light flavour of crab meat. Your local fishmonger will only be sourcing crab from the British coast. It is a crustacean that truly thrives in our waters, still traditionally caught with only those over a certain size taken away for consumption. Vichyssoise has a fancy name, but this chilled soup is a staple of traditional French kitchens. White asparagus – earthier than green asparagus thanks to being force-grown – adds a little sharpness when lightly pickled without being acidic, ensuring that it's still the crab meat doing the heavy lifting here.

For the vichyssoise

100g unsalted butter
350g leeks, white parts only, sliced
350g potatoes, peeled and diced
1 litre vegetable stock
200g watercress, stems removed
250g double cream
Sea salt

For the white asparagus

200g white asparagus, woody parts removed and peeled into ribbons
300ml pickling liquor (see page 249)

For the crab

600g picked white crab meat
1 small bunch of dill, finely chopped
1 small bunch of chervil, finely chopped
1 lemon, zested

For the vichyssoise

In a large saucepan, melt the butter over a medium heat. Add the leeks and cook until softened, stirring occasionally. Add the diced potatoes and stir to combine, cooking for 2-3 minutes. Pour in the vegetable stock and bring to the boil, then reduce to a simmer and cook until the potatoes are tender, about 20 minutes. Remove the pan from the heat and let it cool for a few minutes. Add the watercress to the pot and stir until wilted. Add the cream, then pour the mixture into a large bowl set over iced water, stirring to cool it quickly. Use an immersion blender or transfer the soup to a blender and purée until smooth, then pass through a sieve and season with sea salt to taste. Store in an airtight container in the fridge until needed.

For the white asparagus

Place the white asparagus ribbons into an airtight container and cover with the pickling liquor. This is a short pickle, so after 3 hours, strain off and pat the asparagus dry ready to be served.

For the crab and to serve

In a mixing bowl, combine the white crab meat gently with the chopped herbs and lemon zest, then season with sea salt to taste. Chill your serving bowls in the freezer for 10 minutes, then ladle the chilled vichyssoise into the bowls, add the seasoned crab meat, and finally place the pickled white asparagus on top.

ASPARAGUS, POACHED EGG, CAFÉ DE PARIS EMULSION

SERVES 4

The first delivery of new season asparagus is a key highlight of the British food calendar: a sign of better things to come, a metaphor for change, and we celebrate its arrival religiously, making the most of its short season. As such, this has become something of a seasonal signature at the pub, and it may be my favourite starter we've ever done. My take on a hollandaise features the flavours of the famous Café de Paris butter; though the original recipe and café are now sadly lost to time, it is a decadent sauce of complex flavour that goes well with so much. I enjoy it with this asparagus, and even more so alongside charcoal roast beef.

12 English asparagus spears
50ml white wine vinegar
50g unsalted butter
4 free-range eggs

For the Café de Paris emulsion
50ml egg yolk
50ml apple juice
25ml cider vinegar
½ tbsp Henderson's Relish or Worcestershire sauce
½ tsp English mustard
½ tsp smoked paprika
½ tsp curry powder
½ tsp garlic powder
A tiny pinch of cayenne pepper
A pinch of sea salt
250ml rapeseed oil
½ lemon, juiced
1 shallot, finely diced
1 tbsp chopped chives
½ tbsp lilliput capers
½ tbsp chopped chervil
½ tbsp chopped curly parsley

You can make the emulsion in advance as it will remain stable in the fridge for a few days. Put the egg yolk, apple juice, cider vinegar, Henderson's Relish, mustard, paprika, curry powder, garlic powder, cayenne, and salt into a food processor. Blitz on a continual medium speed to combine, then keep blitzing while slowly adding the rapeseed oil to form a smooth emulsion, pausing halfway through to add the lemon juice. Pour the emulsion into a container and set aside in the fridge until you need it.

Remove the woody ends from the asparagus spears by snapping them off at the natural breaking point. Take a small knife and carefully run the blade lightly around the spear 2cm from the base, then use a vegetable peeler to gently remove the skin below this incision. This ensures that any hard and unpalatable woodiness is completely removed. Heat a large pan of boiling water on the hob and using a colander, steam your asparagus spears for 2 minutes, then cool immediately over iced water.

Keep the water boiling as you can use this to poach your eggs. Season the water with salt and add the white wine vinegar.

Take another small saucepan and gently reheat most of the Café de Paris emulsion, leaving a little in reserve. Add the shallot, chives, capers, chervil, and parsley. Don't let the emulsion boil, otherwise it will split. If it does split, stir in the reserved emulsion. If that doesn't fix it, a splash of ice cold water will do the trick.

Melt the butter in a frying pan, then add the steamed asparagus. Season with salt and turn regularly. Meanwhile, break your eggs into the pan of boiling water with vinegar. Turn the heat down to a medium simmer and cook for 3 minutes 30 seconds. Remove the poached eggs with a slotted spoon and pat dry.

Plate the asparagus, followed by the poached egg, and coat in the emulsion. Enjoy with toast, or – as we do in the restaurant – shaved white truffle.

ST GEORGE'S MUSHROOMS AU GRATIN, WILD GARLIC GRISSINI

SERVES 6

St George's mushrooms – as the name suggests – arrive at our kitchen around late April every year. Often found on grassy patches underneath trees, these off-white mushrooms have a true mushroomy flavour which is earthy and moreish, without that kind of mealy, damp taste some mushrooms can have. Combined with what I regard as the ultimate cheese sauce, this is a great springtime dinner party starter, or even a side dish for something more flamboyant. Please take care when foraging and consult an expert before consuming any foraged mushrooms.

For the grissini

30g wild garlic leaves, chopped
75ml whole milk
1 egg
250g plain flour
A pinch of sea salt

For the crumb

250g stale bread, blitzed to a crumb
75ml extra virgin rapeseed oil
6 cloves of garlic, grated
A pinch of sea salt

For the mushrooms

Rapeseed oil
1 onion, thinly sliced
4 cloves of garlic, thinly sliced
4 sprigs of thyme, leaves picked
1kg St George's mushrooms, cleaned and roughly chopped

For the cheese sauce

50g unsalted butter
50g plain flour
500ml whole milk
1 bay leaf
200g mozzarella block, diced
100g Lincolnshire Poacher
80g Ogleshield, grated
Chopped chives, to garnish (optional)

You can make the grissini and crumb the day before serving this dish.

For the grissini

Preheat your oven to 200°c. Place all the ingredients in a mixing bowl and bring together to form a smooth dough, kneading for around 2 minutes. Shape into a ball, wrap the dough in cling film and place in the fridge for 30 minutes. Roll out the chilled dough to 3mm thickness. Cut into long strips of 1cm width and place on a lined baking tray, then bake in the preheated oven for 15 minutes. Remove from the oven and store in an airtight container once cooled.

For the crumb

Turn the oven temperature down to 150°c. Place all the ingredients in a bowl and mix thoroughly, then spread thinly over a non-stick baking tray. Bake in the oven for 15 minutes or until golden brown, then remove and leave to cool before storing in an airtight container.

For the mushrooms

Heat a little rapeseed oil in a large frying pan on a medium heat. Once hot, add the onion and cook until golden, then add the garlic, thyme, mushrooms, and a pinch of salt. Fry on a medium heat, stirring regularly until most of the water from the mushrooms has been removed, then set aside.

For the cheese sauce

Melt the butter on a low heat in a large saucepan. Once melted, stir in the flour. Allow the flour to cook out for a minute, stirring to ensure it doesn't stick. Add the milk 100ml at a time, stirring as you go until it has all been absorbed into the flour and butter paste. Add the bay leaf and simmer the sauce for a minute, stirring as it begins to thicken, then add all the cheeses. Keep stirring until they melt completely into the sauce.

To assemble

Preheat your oven to 180°c. Add the cooked mushroom mixture to the cheese sauce, stir well and then spoon into suitable ovenproof dishes. Top generously with the crumb, then bake in the oven for 10 minutes. Serve the gratin alongside the grissini, finished with a handful of chopped chives if you wish.

RACK OF LAMB, PRESSED LAMB SHOULDER POTATO, PICKLED MORELS

SERVES 6

This is something of a signature dish throughout spring at The Pack Horse, and it is one of the more technical, busy recipes in this book but has become such a classic that I couldn't leave it out. The pickled morel mushrooms bring an earthy sharpness to this dish, hidden among fresh sea vegetables atop layered potatoes filled with braised lamb shoulder. It takes time but is worth the effort.

For the pickled morels
200g morels, sliced widthways
350ml pickling liquor (see page 249)

For the pressed potato
1kg lamb shoulder, boned and rolled
8 cloves of garlic, peeled and sliced
12 salted anchovy fillets
1 tbsp each runny honey & mint sauce
Sea salt
Rapeseed oil
100g lamb fat
100g unsalted butter
6 large Rooster or Maris Piper potatoes, thinly sliced on a mandoline

For the lamb sauce
2 sticks of celery, diced
1 carrot & 1 onion, diced
1 bay leaf
6 mint stems
125ml Madeira
300ml lamb stock
300ml beef or veal stock

For the lamb rack and sea vegetables
6 x 3-bone lamb racks, French trimmed and skin scored
250g assorted sea vegetables, washed and patted dry

A few days in advance, place the sliced morels in an airtight container and cover with the pickling liquor. Seal with a lid and leave in the fridge until needed.

Assemble the pressed potato a day in advance. Preheat your oven to 240°c. Make small incisions in the lamb shoulder and stud it with the garlic and anchovies, then rub with the honey and mint sauce. Place in a roasting tin, season with salt and rapeseed oil, then place in the preheated oven for 15 minutes. Remove and turn the oven temperature down to 150°c. Add a small glass of water to the tin, then loosely cover with tin foil. Place back in the oven for 2-3 hours until the meat is soft and yielding. Once cool enough to handle, shred the meat with your hands and stir through a little of the cooking liquor from the tin, then set aside. Line another roasting tin with baking parchment. Melt the lamb fat and butter in a saucepan, seasoning with salt. Layer the potatoes in the roasting tin, brushing each layer with the lamb fat mix. Halfway through, add a 0.5cm layer of the shoulder meat. Brush this with the lamb fat mix, then repeat layering and brushing the potatoes until the tin is almost full. Cover with baking parchment and place in the oven at 170°c for 1 hour 30 minutes. Once baked, place a heavy weight on top and leave in the fridge overnight. The following morning, carefully take it out of the tin by running a knife around the edges, then slice into portions.

Fry the celery, carrot, onion, bay, and mint stems for the lamb sauce in rapeseed oil on a high heat until dark and caramelised. Add the Madeira and bring to the boil, reducing it by three quarters. Add the lamb stock, bring back to the boil, reduce by half and then repeat this process with the beef stock. Strain off the vegetables and skim the sauce of any impurities that have risen to the top, then continue to cook until it has a glossy, thick viscosity.

Preheat your oven to 180°c. Heat a frying pan on the hob and then add the lamb racks fat side down. Cook for 2-3 minutes on a high heat to render the fat, then turn the heat down and brown the meat all over. Transfer to a baking tray, leaving the fat in the pan, and roast the racks in the oven for 12-14 minutes. Remove and rest for 10 minutes before carving.

Keep the pan of fat on the heat and fry the pressed potato portions in it until golden and crispy. Heat a small saucepan with around 5mm of water and a knob of unsalted butter in, then add the sea vegetables and cook for 2-3 minutes, seasoning as you go. Drain and serve atop the potato portions, along with 6-8 pickled morels. Carve the lamb racks, following the bone, and place next to the pressed potato, then finish with the lamb sauce.

BEEF & PICKLED WALNUT STEW, NETTLE DUMPLINGS

SERVES 6

This is the perfect stew for one of those spring days where it suddenly turns very cold and wet. Nettles are abundant from April, but make sure to pick the tops only and not ones near pavement edges. Their iron-rich umami flavour plays perfectly with rich, fatty shin beef and sharp pickled walnuts. Opies are the best brand of pickled walnuts, and we always have a jar or three in the fridge. Shin beef can be tough to cut without the correct tools, so ask your butcher to do this for you.

For the stew

1kg shin beef, diced into 4cm cubes
100g plain flour, seasoned with salt
Vegetable oil
2 onions, thinly sliced
2 sticks of celery, finely diced
4 cloves of garlic, peeled and thinly sliced
250g smoked bacon, cut into 2cm cubes
4 sprigs of thyme
2 bay leaves
5 pickled walnuts and their brine
750ml red wine
300ml beef stock or water

For the dumplings

100g nettle tops
250g self-raising flour
125g beef suet
Sea salt
Freshly ground black pepper

For the stew

Toss the diced beef through the seasoned flour until it is coated evenly. Set a heavy-based pan on a medium heat and add the oil, then fry the coated beef until browned all over. Remove from the pan and set aside. Preheat your oven to 150°c.

Add a touch more oil to the pan along with the onion, celery, garlic, bacon, thyme, and bay. Cook until golden and then add the pickled walnut brine, turning up the heat to quickly reduce this to a thin syrup, while scraping all the residue from the base of the pan.

Add the browned beef and the pickled walnuts, letting them break up naturally as you stir. Pour in the wine and bring to the boil, allowing the wine to reduce by half, then finally add the stock. Boil for 10 minutes, then cover with a lid and place in the oven for 2 hours 30 minutes, stirring occasionally.

For the dumplings

Bring a pan of water to the boil and then add the nettle tops. Cook for 2 minutes until wilted, then drain but keep 200ml of the water for the dumpling mix. Cool the nettles quickly over ice to retain their colour. Once cooked, they will not sting you. Squeeze the water from the nettle leaves and chop them up finely.

In a mixing bowl, combine the flour and suet. Season with salt and pepper, then add the chopped nettle leaves. Slowly add the nettle water to the bowl and mix gently to bring everything together until you have a soft dough (you may not need all the water).

Shape the dumplings into 10 spheres and place on top of the bubbling stew. Cover the pan once more with the lid, place back in the oven and cook for another 20-25 minutes before serving.

TURBOT POACHED ON THE BONE, WHITE ASPARAGUS, MORELS, SAUCE BONNE FEMME

SERVES 4

This recipe may sound a little daunting but if you have the ingredients to hand, it can be surprisingly quick and easy to accomplish. Turbot is a fish simply unrivalled for its taste and texture, and our take on a classic sauce bonne femme adds the richness and decadence that turbot deserves.

6 white asparagus spears, trimmed and halved lengthways

Rapeseed oil

Sea salt

1 litre fish stock

2 shallots, thinly sliced

250g morel mushrooms

125ml Madeira

3 tbsp soy sauce

1 tbsp fish sauce

300ml fish or chicken stock

100ml double cream

50g wild garlic, shredded

4 x 200g pieces of turbot, tranche-cut on the bone

Preheat your oven to 170°c. Line up the halved asparagus on a baking tray, then drizzle with rapeseed oil and season with salt to taste.

Bring the litre of fish stock to a boil in a large saucepan, then reduce to a simmer and cover with a lid.

In another saucepan, heat a little rapeseed oil and add the shallot, cooking on a low heat until golden. Add the morels and cook until soft, then add the Madeira, soy sauce, and fish sauce. Bring to the boil and reduce the volume of liquid by about two thirds, then add the fish or chicken stock.

Boil and reduce the morel sauce by half before finishing with the double cream, then leave it on a gentle simmer until needed. Add the wild garlic just before serving and allow to cook for 1 minute in the hot sauce.

Meanwhile, place the asparagus in the preheated oven and roast for 10 minutes until soft and lightly caramelised. Place the turbot portions into the large pan of hot fish stock and cover with a lid, turning the heat up to medium. Poach the turbot for 10 minutes. If you have a meat thermometer, 48°c directly on the bone is ideal. Remove the turbot from the stock with a fish slice and pat dry with a cloth, then serve atop the roasted asparagus and sauce bonne femme.

BREADED WHOLE PLAICE, MUSHY PEAS, CHIP SHOP CURRY SAUCE

SERVES 4

My love for cooking fish on the bone seemingly knows no bounds, as during the summer of 2021 I decided to shock just about everyone that works with us and do a whole fish breaded and deep fried. It worked a treat. Delicate plaice needs a confident and steady hand to cook well, so the layer of breadcrumbs and cooking it on the bone add double protection. Traditional chip shop garniture brings a sense of comfort and familiarity to an otherwise unusual take on the nation's favourite.

4 x 400-600g whole plaice, gutted and fins removed

150g plain flour

8 eggs, beaten

250g panko breadcrumbs

200ml rapeseed or sunflower oil

Lemon wedges, to serve

For the mushy peas

400g dried marrowfat peas

50g unsalted butter

1 shallot, finely chopped

1 clove of garlic, minced

1 tsp ground white pepper

Sea salt

For the curry sauce

50g unsalted butter

50g plain flour

2 tbsp curry powder

400ml chicken stock

1 cardamom pod

1 star anise

100ml double cream

2 tsp white wine vinegar

1 tsp caster sugar

For the mushy peas

Rinse the dried marrowfat peas in a colander and place them in a large bowl. Cover with water and let them soak overnight. The next day, drain the peas and place them in a large saucepan. Cover with fresh water and bring to the boil over a medium-high heat, then reduce to a simmer for about 60-90 minutes, or until they are very tender and falling apart. Drain the peas and return them to the saucepan. Add the butter, chopped shallot, minced garlic, and ground white pepper to the peas and stir well to combine. Cook the mixture over a low heat for 5-10 minutes, or until the shallot and garlic are softened, stirring often to ensure nothing sticks. Use a potato masher or immersion blender to mash the peas until they reach your desired consistency, adding water to loosen if needed, and season to taste with sea salt.

For the curry sauce

Melt the butter in a saucepan over a medium heat. Add the flour and curry powder and whisk continuously for 1-2 minutes, until the mixture is smooth and fragrant. Gradually pour in the chicken stock, whisking constantly to avoid lumps. Add the cardamom and star anise, then bring the mixture to the boil, reduce the heat and simmer for 10-15 minutes, stirring occasionally, until the sauce thickens. Add the double cream to the saucepan and stir until well combined. Finally, stir in the white wine vinegar and sugar, then season to taste with sea salt. Simmer for a further 5-10 minutes, stirring occasionally, until the sauce is heated through and has reached your desired consistency.

Put the flour, beaten egg, and breadcrumbs in 3 separate large, shallow containers. Coat the plaice in the flour and tap off any excess, then place into the beaten egg and turn to ensure the fish is fully coated. Let the excess drip off and transfer to the breadcrumbs, again ensuring it's fully coated. Heat the oil in a very large, wide frying pan. Once the oil is hot, place the fish in the oil carefully and fry on each side for 5 minutes, then transfer to a baking tray and pat dry. Serve alongside the warm mushy peas and curry sauce with a sprinkling of sea salt and some lemon wedges.

JERSEY ROYALS FRIED IN SEAWEED VINEGAR, PURPLE SPROUTING BROCCOLI, LOVAGE PESTO, GOAT'S CURD

SERVES 6

This makes a great vegetarian main course on its own but can also accompany all kinds of meat and fish as a sharing salad. Our Jersey Royals first arrive at the pub in early April, specially selected for us from an organic producer who fertilises the soil with seaweed. We've leant on that flavour profile with a simple seaweed vinegar to add a sharp umami kick. Lovage – a love it or hate it herb – adds a peppery, celery-like savouriness to a classic pesto.

For the seaweed vinegar

750ml cider vinegar
20g dried wakame
20g dried kelp
¼ tsp chilli flakes

For the lovage pesto

200g lovage leaves
150g pine nuts
150g Spenwood or parmesan
2 cloves of garlic
1 lemon, juiced
350ml extra virgin olive oil
Sea salt

For the salad

1kg Jersey Royals, cleaned and scrubbed
500g purple sprouting broccoli, trimmed
300g spring onions, washed and cut into thirds
300g goat's curd
Rapeseed oil
Unsalted butter

For the seaweed vinegar

This makes more than you need for this recipe, but it's a lovely ingredient to have lying around as it keeps for a long time. A few weeks before making the dish, place the vinegar, seaweeds and chilli flakes into a sterilised airtight jar and leave to infuse for 2-3 weeks.

For the lovage pesto

Place all the ingredients apart from the oil and salt into a food processor. Blitz to form a paste, then trickle the oil in gradually as it continues to blitz. Season to taste and keep in the fridge until needed.

For the salad

Place the Jersey Royals in a pan of water seasoned with salt and bring to a boil. Boil for 20 minutes or until the potatoes are soft, then drain and cool immediately under cold running water. Halve the Jerseys with a knife and set to one side.

Put a frying on a medium heat and heat a little rapeseed oil. Once hot, add the halved potatoes, purple sprouting broccoli and spring onion to fry on a medium heat for 8 minutes, tossing and stirring as you go. A little colour on the vegetables is ideal.

With the pan still hot, add a good glug of your seaweed vinegar and turn the heat up, stirring continuously. As soon as all the vinegar has evaporated, add a knob of unsalted butter and once that has melted, plate up. Drizzle over the lovage pesto and top with a few spoonfuls of the goat's curd.

ROAST LAMB LEG WITH ANCHOVIES, CAPERS, ROSEMARY & MINT

SERVES 6-8

This is a great feasting joint, and a wonderful table centrepiece for an Easter roast. Anchovies are a Marmite ingredient, but I urge you all to embrace them, especially with lamb. A good quality salted anchovy isn't fishy; it carries an intense punch of well-rounded savoury flavour. When you've tried them in this marinade, I can guarantee you'll always have a jar to hand in the cupboard.

1 bone-in lamb leg weighing 2-3kg
18 salted anchovy fillets
2 tbsp capers
4 cloves of garlic
2 sprigs of rosemary
1 bunch of mint leaves
1 tbsp runny honey
1 tbsp white wine vinegar
1 tbsp rapeseed or vegetable oil
1 tsp wholegrain mustard
Sea salt
175ml white wine

On a chopping board, score the skin of the lamb leg with a knife just deep enough to open the flesh slightly, and place into a roasting tin.

Roughly chop the anchovy fillets, capers and garlic, then place in a mixing bowl. Add the rosemary leaves and roughly tear in half of the mint leaves. Add the honey, vinegar, oil, and mustard as well as a good pinch of salt, then mix to combine evenly.

Rub this mixture evenly all over the lamb leg, ensuring it is pushed into the score marks. Preheat your oven to 220°c while the lamb marinates for half an hour to an hour.

Place the marinated lamb in the oven for 25 minutes, then remove and turn the oven down to 160°c. Thoroughly baste the lamb leg, then add the white wine to the tin and place back in the oven for between 50 minutes and 2 hours depending on how you like your lamb cooked.

Remove the lamb from the oven and pour the juices into a saucepan, then loosely cover the lamb leg and leave to rest for 20 minutes.

Leave the pan of juices for 5 minutes, allowing the lamb fat to rise to the top. Using a spoon or ladle, skim the fat away from the juices and pour into a plastic container – it's always good to keep lamb fat for future roasts. You have options for the remaining roasting juices; add to our gravy recipe (see page 242) for something more traditional or serve as it is for something lighter. Either way, tear in the remaining mint leaves just before serving and give it a good stir to make sure the chopped capers and anchovies don't sit in the bottom of the jug.

The bone should yield comfortably from a lamb leg cooked well-done, making carving easier. Personally, I prefer my lamb leg cooked medium, enough to render the fat but ensuring a delicious blush pink colour. To carve at medium, take slices following the direction of the bone.

WILD RABBIT, TROTTER & MUSTARD PIE

SERVES 6

I love rabbit and it's a meat we could all do with eating more of. Not only are rabbits plentiful, but they are pests to farmers growing vegetables and can easily decimate fields of crops. On top of that, their meat is lean, rich in protein, and given its totally wild lifestyle, very flavoursome. Braised here with unctuous, fatty trotter meat and a dollop of mustard, it might be my favourite pie filling. As with the other pie recipes in this book, the choice of pastry is entirely up to you, with recipes on page 250.

1 whole 1.5-2kg oven-ready wild rabbit

6 pig's trotters

2.5 litres trotter stock (see page 249)

3 leeks, white parts only, thinly sliced

2 sticks of celery, finely diced

1 bay leaf

125ml Madeira

100g crème fraiche

50g wholegrain mustard

1 tbsp English mustard

500g pie pastry (I recommend hot water pastry)

2 egg yolks, beaten

Rapeseed oil

Sea salt

Place the rabbit and trotters in a large saucepan and cover with the trotter stock. Bring to the boil, then turn down to a simmer and cover. Allow to cook for 2-3 hours until the meat is soft and yielding.

Remove the meat from the stock and set aside. Keep the stock on a strong boil and reduce the volume of liquid by two thirds. Once cool enough to handle, pick the rabbit and trotter meat from the bones.

Heat a little rapeseed oil in a large saucepan and add the leek, celery and bay once hot. Sweat on a low heat until translucent. Season with a little salt, add the rabbit and trotter meat, then add the Madeira and turn the heat up to a boil. Reduce the liquid by half, then pour in just enough of the reduced trotter stock to cover everything. Stir in the crème fraiche and both mustards, then cook the filling for a further 10 minutes.

Lightly grease a 20cm pie tin with butter and roll your pastry out to 3mm thickness. Lay the pastry into the tin, pressing it gently into the sides all the way around. Chill in the fridge for 30 minutes.

Fill the pie tin with the rabbit mix and cut out a lid from the remaining pastry. Crimp this onto the pie and then brush thoroughly with the egg yolk. Place in a preheated oven at 190°c for 30 minutes and then serve with accompaniments of your choice.

CHICKEN RUBY

SERVES 6

Indian food remains one of the nation's favourite cuisines, and our weekly Wednesday quiz night revolves around curries. The chicken ruby – our take on the Dishoom classic, adapted from a traditional makhani and aptly named after the cockney rhyming slang – is better than anything you'll get in a takeaway. Although time consuming, I can guarantee it'll change your perspective of what good Indian food really is. Our favourite curry accompaniments can be found towards the back of this book on pages 252 and 253, it's worth serving them all with this curry for a true Indian feast at home.

For the chicken

1.2kg skinless and boneless chicken thighs

3 tbsp garlic and ginger paste

1 tbsp ground cumin

1 tsp garam masala

1 tsp chilli powder

10g sea salt

2 limes, juiced

150g natural yoghurt

50g unsalted butter, melted

For the sauce

200ml vegetable oil

6 cloves of garlic, thinly sliced

8 green cardamom pods

2 black cardamom pods

2 cinnamon sticks

2 bay leaves

3 tbsp garlic and ginger paste

3 x 400g tins of plum tomatoes

6 dried fenugreek leaves

2 tsp ground cumin

2 tsp deggi mirch chilli powder

60g unsalted butter

1½ tbsp runny honey

1½ tsp garam masala

½ tsp finely chopped dill

150ml double cream

For the chicken

Begin by marinating the chicken thighs. The longer you leave them the better, so I'd recommend preparing them the night before. Combine all the ingredients except the butter in a large mixing bowl and stir thoroughly to ensure all the chicken thighs have an even coating. Cover with cling film and place in the fridge to marinate overnight.

The following day, heat your oven to its highest temperature setting. Spread the chicken thighs out across a few baking trays, leaving space between them. Lightly brush with the melted butter and roast for 10-15 minutes until the chicken is cooked and the marinade is charred on the outside. Remove and leave to cool. Once cool enough to handle, cut the chicken thighs into 4cm pieces and store in the fridge until needed.

For the sauce

Warm the oil in a large saucepan over a medium-high heat. Add the sliced garlic and fry until light golden brown. Remove immediately with a slotted spoon and drain on a piece of kitchen roll. Carefully drop the cardamom pods, cinnamon sticks and bay leaves into the hot oil and fry for a minute, stirring regularly.

Add the garlic and ginger paste to the pan of spices and fry for a minute, allowing it to brown slightly. Add the plum tomatoes, fenugreek leaves, cumin, chilli powder, and sea salt to taste. Stir to combine everything, bring to the boil, and reduce the volume by half. This does have a tendency to catch, so keep stirring and scraping the pan as the sauce reduces. Be prepared to transfer pans if it does catch, otherwise the burnt flavour will taint the sauce.

Once reduced, add the butter, honey, garam masala, and dill to the sauce. Stir well and cook for a further 20 minutes. Now add the double cream and simmer on a low heat for 10 minutes, then add the chicken pieces and all the charred marinade. Allow the chicken to simmer in the sauce for 15 minutes before serving with all your accompaniments.

GIN & TONIC CHEESECAKE, CUCUMBER GRANITA

SERVES 6

What's not to love about a boozy cheesecake? Imagine being sat in a garden in full bloom enjoying the first alfresco dining of the year, tucking into a dessert with all the refreshing flavours of your favourite gin and tonic. The cucumber granita just takes the edge off, and even makes a lovely refresher on its own during those first warm days of long sunshine.

1 large cucumber
100ml elderflower tonic
75ml cold water
2 limes, juiced
1 bunch of fresh mint, leaves only
¼ tsp fine sea salt
150g digestive biscuits
75g unsalted butter
4 gelatine leaves
300g cream cheese
100g mascarpone
150ml double cream
100g caster sugar
100ml gin
50ml tonic water
1 lime, zested

Finely dice the cucumber and transfer to a food processor with the elderflower tonic, cold water, lime juice, mint leaves, and salt. Process until the mixture is smooth, then pour it into an airtight container. Cover and freeze for 45 minutes, then stir and scrape with a fork and freeze again. Repeat this process over about 3 hours until the mixture is completely icy.

Using a rolling pin, crush the digestive biscuits until they resemble breadcrumbs. Gently melt the butter on a low heat and then combine it with the biscuit crumbs. Press the biscuit mixture into the bottom of a 20cm springform cake tin, using the back of a spoon to smooth and level the mixture. Chill in the fridge while you prepare the filling.

Place the gelatine leaves in a bowl of cold water and leave to soak for 5 minutes. In a mixing bowl, whisk the cream cheese, mascarpone, double cream, and caster sugar together until smooth.

In a small saucepan, heat the gin and tonic water over a medium heat until it begins to simmer. Remove from the heat and stir in the lime zest. Remove the gelatine leaves from the water and squeeze out the excess liquid, then add them to the saucepan. Stir until the gelatine has dissolved and then pour into the cream cheese mixture, whisking to combine them thoroughly.

Pour the cheesecake mixture over the biscuit base and smooth the top with a spatula. Chill in the fridge for at least 2 hours, or until firm. Scrape the granita with a fork one final time, then slice the cheesecake and plate up, serving with the granita fresh from the freezer.

VANILLA CRÈME BRULÉE, PINK PEPPERCORN SHORTBREAD

SERVES 6

I've always been very fond of the traditional brulée, and this was the first dessert I made in-house after buying in some disastrous traybake desserts for our opening menus. It's become a mainstay on the menu ever since, a real dark horse. The pink peppercorns in the shortbread add a much-needed fiery hit to break through the sweet richness of the cream.

For the shortbread

250g diced butter, at room temperature
100g caster sugar
280g plain flour
1 tbsp pink peppercorns

For the brulée

75g caster sugar
9 egg yolks (160ml)
450ml double cream
1 tsp vanilla paste
Granulated sugar, for caramelising

For the shortbread

In a mixing bowl, beat the butter and sugar together, then sift over the flour. Stir to combine until the mixture resembles fine breadcrumbs. Add the pink peppercorns and bring the mix together.

Lay a piece of cling film out on your bench and shape the dough into a rough log, then roll it firmly in the cling film to create a tightly set log shape. Place in the fridge for an hour to firm up.

Preheat your oven to 165°c. Remove the cling film from the chilled dough and cut the log into rounds roughly 1.5cm thick. Spread these out evenly on a baking tray lined with greaseproof paper, leaving at least an inch between each one. Place in the preheated oven for 15 minutes, remove and dust with a little more caster sugar, then leave to cool. Once cool, transfer to an airtight container.

For the brulée

Preheat your oven to 100°c and line up 6 ovenproof ramekins in a roasting tin. Fill the tin with enough boiling water to come halfway up the ramekins.

In a mixing bowl, lightly beat the sugar and egg yolks together. Place the cream and vanilla paste into a saucepan and bring to the boil on a medium heat, whisking occasionally to ensure the vanilla is combining properly. Once boiling, slowly pour the vanilla cream over the egg yolk and sugar mix, whisking continuously to avoid it scrambling. Once combined, use a ladle to skim off the thick layer of bubbles which has formed on the top.

Evenly distribute the custard mixture between the ramekins and carefully place in your preheated oven. Bake for 25 minutes or until set (a slight wobble is perfect). Remove from the oven, take the ramekins out of the roasting tin and leave to cool at room temperature before placing in the fridge.

When ready to serve, remove your brulées from the fridge and evenly dust the top with granulated sugar. Using a cook's blowtorch, caramelise the sugar carefully and evenly to a golden brown colour. Serve alongside the shortbread.

GARDEN RHUBARB CRUMBLE, VANILLA CUSTARD

SERVES 4

Just as the final spears of hot-pink forced rhubarb come through the kitchen doors, garden rhubarb season begins. A more maroon/green colour, the outdoor rhubarb is however just as sharp as its shed-grown counterparts. It stews down beautifully into a rustic crumble, made here with gluten-free buckwheat flour which has a lovely nutty flavour. You can be flexible with the amount of sugar, but I like my rhubarb sharp to cut through the richness of the vanilla custard.

For the filling

500g garden rhubarb
100g caster sugar
50ml water

For the topping

150g buckwheat flour
90g unsalted butter, cubed and chilled
60g demerara sugar

For the custard

250g whole milk
250g double cream
1 vanilla pod, split lengthways
4 egg yolks (60ml)
50g caster sugar
1 tsp cornflour

For the filling

Cut the rhubarb into thumb-sized pieces. Place a pan with a suitable lid on a medium heat and cook the rhubarb in the sugar and water until just beginning to break down a little, stirring it as you go. Transfer the filling to an ovenproof dish and preheat your oven to 180°c.

For the topping

Put all the ingredients in a mixing bowl and bring together by rubbing them between your fingers until the mixture resembles fine breadcrumbs. Scatter this evenly over the rhubarb and then place the crumble in your preheated oven for 30 minutes.

For the custard

Make this while the crumble bakes. Pour the milk and cream into a saucepan. Scrape the vanilla seeds from the split pod and add these too. Gently warm until it just begins to boil.

In a mixing bowl, combine the egg yolks, caster sugar and cornflour. Just as the cream comes to the boil, pour it over the egg mixture and whisk to combine.

Transfer the custard back to the pan and reheat very slowly, whisking continuously until it begins to thicken, for around 10 minutes. If the custard splits, add a tablespoon of iced water and whisk again.

Serve the custard alongside your hot crumble fresh from the oven.

CHOCOLATE & PEANUT BUTTER DELICE, HONEYCOMB, BLOOD ORANGE ICE CREAM

SERVES 8

This is my favourite chocolate dessert, and we are often asked when it's coming back onto the menu. At home, it's a show-stopping dessert fit for a feast but does require some forward planning and specialist equipment: a sugar thermometer is a must, as well as a large bottomless tart ring or rectangular baking mould. Be careful with honeycomb; it reaches such a high temperature and is volcanic when the bicarbonate of soda is introduced.

For the honeycomb
150g caster sugar
50g golden syrup
50g liquid glucose
22g bicarbonate of soda

For the ice cream
300ml double cream
200ml whole milk
100g caster sugar
3 egg yolks (60ml)
2 blood oranges, juiced

For the delice
100g cornflakes
200g peanut butter
120ml whole milk
350ml double cream
350g dark chocolate
3 eggs

For the honeycomb

You can make this in advance and store it for up to 3 days. First, line a roasting tin with baking parchment. Combine the sugar, syrup and glucose in a heavy-based saucepan on a medium heat and bring the temperature of the mixture to precisely 142°c. Remove from the heat instantly at this point, then add the bicarbonate of soda and whisk to combine. The mixture will expand rapidly, so carefully pour it straight into the lined roasting tin and leave to cool. Once cool and set, tip the honeycomb onto a chopping board and cut into cubes. It will keep in an airtight container for 3 days.

For the ice cream

Make this the day before you want to serve the dessert, along with your delice. Add the cream and milk to a pan and bring to the boil. In a mixing bowl, beat the sugar and egg yolks together. Pour the boiling cream mixture into the egg mixture, whisking continuously, then add the blood orange juice and whisk to combine. Pour the mixture back into the pan and heat until it reaches precisely 82°c, then transfer it to a suitable container with a lid. Leave to cool overnight. Churn the chilled custard in the ice cream machine first thing in the morning, then transfer to the freezer and leave to set.

For the delice

In a food processor, blitz the cornflakes and peanut butter to a smooth paste. Line your tart ring or mould with baking parchment and spread the paste evenly inside it to create a flat base, ensuring there are no holes or gaps. Place in the fridge for an hour to chill and set.

Bring the milk and cream to the boil on a medium heat. Finely chop the chocolate and place in a heatproof mixing bowl. Once the cream mixture is boiling, remove it from the heat and break in the eggs, whisking to combine, and then pour this over the chopped chocolate. Whisk until the chocolate has fully melted and you have a smooth paste. Pour this over the set cornflake base and place in the fridge overnight.

Once the delice has set, slice it into rectangular portions and serve with a few pieces of honeycomb and a spoonful of ice cream.

A DAY AT THE PACK HORSE

It was Gordon Ramsay who once said that "running a restaurant is like putting on a live show every day – but without a script" and he's not wrong. Although there is a routine to our actions within the pub, and some familiarity with our guests and what they order, the timing of everything is constantly up in the air. It's a daily balancing act full of twists and surprises, and it is the hard work of the team behind the scenes that ensures the smooth operation of the pub. Even before the workday begins at The Pack Horse, there's plenty already happening. The ovens that have been slowly roasting meats overnight fill the pub with a beautiful and comforting aroma, and the first delivery of vegetables arrives at 7am.

The chefs begin at 8.30, packing deliveries away over a coffee before consulting the mis en place sheet completed the night before, which details everything that each section needs to do. Our kitchen is a small space with a small team, so a loose brigade system is followed with sections split into sauce, larder and pastry. One of the first things in the oven every day is the salted caramel custard tart, as we need to get this set for lunch service so it's still slightly warm when served, which is a real treat for our first guests.

At 10am our bread dough for lunch service is removed from the fridge and given a final proving at room temperature for an hour. The fish delivery then arrives, which is quickly broken down into what we need; portions for service go one way, bones for stock go another, and oysters are checked over and laid neatly in the fridge. The front of house team also begin their preparations for the day, checking booking notes, laying tables, and racking beer barrels for conditioning before serving.

At 11am the energy levels ramp up, knowing that lunchtime is fast approaching. A quick briefing between front and back of house takes place, ensuring any allergies have been flagged up as well as any menu changes. At 11.15, the bread is baked for lunch and the kitchen is cleaned down before setting up each section for service. Around this time our meat delivery arrives, once again taken in different directions according to what we need. On busy days, one chef will be designated to our prep kitchen space, taking the pressure off the rest of the team as they complete jobs for each section. On even busier days, I'll order the team a large pork pie from Mettricks to arrive with the meat delivery, so we all manage to have a hearty snack before lunch service.

The doors open at 12pm and lunch service begins. Typically, we have fewer people booked in at lunch, but being a proper country pub there's always plenty of folk wandering in for a drink or small bite from our bar menu – there's a lovely buzz around the place during this time. Just as the last desserts go out at 2.30, the kitchen team clean down once more. At this point, any top ups required on each section are fulfilled, as well as the room temperature proving of the bread for dinner service. Front of house re-lay the dining tables for the evening, and the stage is set once more.

At 3.30 one of the kitchen team (usually Pedro) breaks off and prepares the staff meal. We do this every day for the team, making sure everyone has had a proper hot meal for the day and feels nourished going into evening service. The bar continues to tick over in the meantime, but as the final kitchen prep is packed away and cleaned down once more, the feeling of nervous excitement before the curtain drops for our final act sets in.

One final section set up for the kitchen, and evening service begins at 5pm. Front of house announce its beginning by lighting the candles around the pub, and the first guests arriving receive their complimentary bread and snacks. Both the kitchen and front of house are in full flow now: a full restaurant rocking to the rhythm of service, with many watchful eyes trained on our chefs in the open kitchen, almost like actors on a stage themselves. The bar, crammed with locals enjoying an evening drink after work, creates a background energy to the intricate ballet performed by front of house, weaving between tables and pouring pints. In that moment – as I'm stood on the pass managing the orders, checking the cookery, and plating the food – I consider Gordon's words, and realise he's right. It is all theatre, being played out in front of us every day with no script. And it is joyous to behold from every perspective. A kitchen team so slick and professional, a front of house team so aware of everything going on around them, and our guests just taking it all in, enjoying their company and the show around them.

At 10pm, the cleaning down begins and the mis en place sheets are completed for the following day. By going through this rigorously, we minimise the chances of missing items and therefore avoid having to adapt or change dishes unnecessarily. The orders are phoned in at the end of service for delivery the next day, and everything is back in its place ready to go tomorrow. By 10.30, the chefs are leaving or enjoying a pint with the remaining locals while front of house set the tables for the following day and clean the bar around our final patrons. By 11.30, the doors are shut, and all is calm. Like none of it ever happened, ready to go again the next morning.

Summer

Summer is a season of transformation. If Spring is setting the scene, Summer brings the first real drama into nature's theatrical four act play. Stifling heatwaves are becoming more common and can quickly turn lush green into dry yellows and browns: all the promise of Spring seemingly undone in a moment by the sun. But, true to British form, our summer storms bring occasionally biblical levels of rain, supplementing an environment about to burst into fruitful plenty.

Juicy ripe strawberries, gooseberries fit to burst, greenhouses overflowing with tomatoes, the fat tubes of bright green courgettes; every plant seems to be offering something to someone. That is Summer's bounty, these bursts of flavour everywhere you look, quite literally the fruits of nature's labour thanks to the hustling insects scrambling from flower to flower throughout early summer, like an invertebrate's Shibuya Crossing among the greenery.

In the kitchen, the flavours lean even more into freshness and lightness. A lot of the summer fruits coming into the kitchen are intentionally left in their purest form to showcase just how good nature has made them, only a sporadic pickling or barbecuing required for most produce. It is a time of plenty and one which we embrace, not least because its unpredictability through extreme heat or rain can quickly bring an end to it all. I implore you to take a walk through your local allotment on a late summer's eve, and take a moment of reflection among the creeping beans and ripening marrows. You will quickly find peace.

Shall I compare thee to a summer's day?
Thou art more lovely and more temperate:
Rough winds do shake the darling buds of May,
And summer's lease hath all too short a date:
Sometime too hot the eye of heaven shines,
And often is his gold complexion dimmed;
And every fair from fair sometime declines,
By chance or nature's changing course untrimmed.

From Sonnet 18, William Shakespeare

OUR SEASONAL HIGHLIGHTS

JUNE	JULY	AUGUST
Gooseberries	Strawberries	Blackcurrants
Raspberries	Tomatoes	Courgettes
Cucumber	Samphire	Sweetcorn
Lettuce	Peas	Damsons

Kinder Reservoir & Twenty Trees

6 MILES, MODERATE, ALLOW 2–3 HOURS.

Beloved local landmarks and views of Kinder. Several moderate climbs; parts may be muddy after rain. A couple of streams which may be awkwardly swollen after exceptionally wet weather- must be forded.

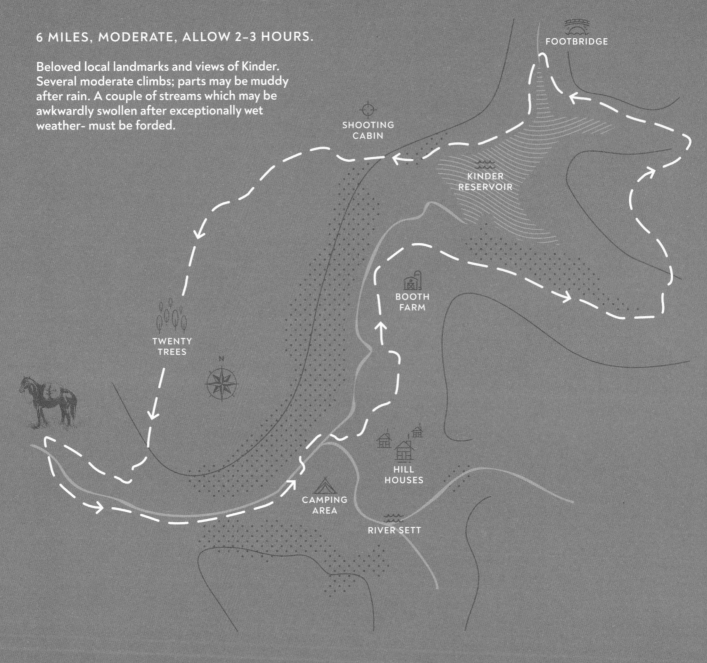

Kinder Reservoir was built between 1903 and 1912 to supply the needs of Stockport Corporation. A short-lived railway line was built up the valley to the site, and the workers lived in a temporary 'tin town' below the dam. The campsite is built on the site of a former textile mill. Twenty Trees is a famous lookout point situated above Hayfield, named after – as you may have guessed – the trees at this location. There are now only 19 trees, however, and the whereabouts of the twentieth has been the subject of much village gossip, which ranges from wondering if there was ever a twentieth tree to knowing the drunkard who cut it down.

From the front door of The Pack Horse, turn left. Bear right over the River Sett and keep left of the church up the main road, Church Street, passing The George Hotel and the fish and chip shop. At the top of Church Street, turn left and left again into Valley Road.

Follow Valley Road, keeping left following the river, but not crossing it. After a row of terraced houses on the right, the path descends to a no-through road. Keep left again at the fork bearing the owl carving, keeping the high stone retaining wall on your right. Descend to the river and after the last houses follow the riverside path, ignoring a footbridge. When the path divides, keep left through the gateposts and walk between the river and the campsite. Keep an eye out for the heron.

Follow to the end of the road at the campsite entrance and turn left over the road bridge, then immediately turn right past Bowden Bridge car park. When the road bends slightly left at Bowden Bridge Cottage, turn right onto the riverside track. At the entrance to Oakbank, turn right over the pack horse bridge. In the corner beyond, turn left through a gate and climb a walled path, then go through another gate and past a converted barn to emerge at Hill Houses.

Turn left past the farmhouse on your left and go through a gate. Follow the track beyond, bending left then right to reach Booth Farm after half a mile. Beyond the farm, descend to a lane and turn right, uphill, passing between the buildings of Farlands. Opposite a bench and path on the left, turn right through a gateway. Follow the track across the field up to the edge of a coniferous plantation on your left. Follow the edge of the wood to its end, ignoring the Oaken Clough bridleway that heads off right at PNFS sign number 285.

Beyond the end of the wood, follow the track ahead to a stile by a gate and National Trust sign, then ford the stream on your left. Cross the National Trust stile and follow the path beyond up the hillside; bear right then left between broken walls to a gate in a more complete wall. Turn left, parallel to the wall, then when the vague track bears left, turn right on a narrow path that descends to meet another wall obliquely. Follow this wall to a junction of walls and then bear right along the obvious descending path that curves left down to a footbridge. Cross the bridge and turn left, taking the higher (right-hand) path that passes above a walled clump of silver birch trees. Bear left along the wall towards the reservoir, leaving it to cross a small stream and then climbing to a hand-gate. The path beyond contours above trees then curves right and descends to a gate. Ford a side-stream and continue to cross the footbridge over William Clough.

Turn left and follow the path above and along the reservoir wall. At a fork, take the right-hand (upper) path that climbs slightly through the heather, leading away from the reservoir. Rejoin the reservoir wall at a hand-gate and continue along the wall, below open woodland. After an information board erected to mark the centenary of the reservoir, level with the dam, turn right, uphill. Follow the path alongside the wall to a gate at the top. Bear left then right across the open moor to a junction of paths below the shooting cabin. Listen out for chatter of grouse among the heather. Turn left (signposted "Hayfield 1½ miles").

Follow the obvious path through the heather to a National Trust sign for the Snake Path. Go through the kissing gate and follow the track across rough grazing land. After a stretch alongside a wall, go through a gate and cross the field, aiming for the treetops of Twenty Trees. Follow the wall and then go through a kissing gate on your right, above the clump of trees. Bear left past the trees to a further kissing gate and commemorative sign. Descend along the bottom of the next field to a gate and stile. Follow the track beyond, which bends left to join a concrete drive and leads down to Kinder Road. Turn right and walk downhill past the library. At the junction with Bank Street, continue ahead along Kinder Road back to The Pack Horse.

ISLE OF WIGHT TOMATOES, BURRATA, PICKLED GARLIC BUDS

SERVES 6

The Isle of Wight gets the most sunshine per year in the whole of the United Kingdom, making it the best place in the country to grow tomatoes. The Tomato Stall set about growing heritage tomatoes on the island almost 20 years ago and are now completely zero waste and organically certified. Their tomatoes are without doubt the most tomatoey I've ever tasted. Served simply as a light summer salad, the different varieties of tomato add complexity in both flavour and texture which belies the simplicity of this dish. Pickled garlic buds, taken from flowering wild garlic in the spring, add a sharp garlicky bite that's well worth the months of preserving.

100g wild garlic buds

250ml pickling liquor (see page 249)

1kg Isle of Wight heritage tomatoes, quartered

2 shallots, finely diced

2 tbsp lilliput capers

Sea salt

100ml tarragon vinegar

300g burrata

The wild garlic buds will need to be gathered in the last week of April, or just before the wild garlic flowers bloom. Pour the pickling liquor over them and store in an airtight container or Kilner jar until required. You may also be able to purchase these from online foragers.

Place the quartered tomatoes in a large mixing bowl. Add the shallots, capers, and a pinch of sea salt, then pour over the vinegar and stir to ensure it covers the tomatoes. Let them sit in the vinegar for 10 minutes, stirring halfway through.

Meanwhile, discard the water from the burrata and tear the cheese into chunks, drying them slightly with a cloth before serving. Drain the tomatoes, keeping a little of the tomatoey vinegar that remains. Spoon the tomatoes into bowls and top with the torn burrata, a little of the vinegar, and a few pickled wild garlic buds. In the restaurant, we also add peppery nasturtium leaves from the garden so you could garnish the salad with these, if you have some.

RAW COURGETTES, FENNEL, HERBS, PUMPKIN SEEDS, MOZZARELLA

SERVES 4

The first courgettes of the summer are a delight, and so often wasted. Pick them young and enjoy them raw with loads of fresh herbs for the easiest and most delicious summer salad. Good mozzarella here is so important; nothing from the supermarkets comes close to the real deal.

120g pumpkin seeds

8 young courgettes, thinly sliced

2 fennel bulbs, thinly sliced

4–5 tbsp extra virgin olive oil

½ lemon, juiced

A handful of mint leaves, roughly torn

1 large buffalo mozzarella, torn into pieces

1 large bunch of dill, roughly picked

Sea salt

Heat a frying pan on the hob. Once hot, add the pumpkin seeds and lightly toast for a minute, then set aside and leave to cool.

Place the sliced courgette and fennel in a mixing bowl and season with salt. Pour over the olive oil and lemon juice, toss through, then add the mint leaves.

Serve the salad in bowls, scattered with the torn mozzarella, dill fronds, and toasted pumpkin seeds.

BBQ MACKEREL, GEM LETTUCE, HORSERADISH RANCH DRESSING, GOOSEBERRY SALSA

SERVES 4

Mackerel is my favourite fish to eat. I love its inherently salty, oily flesh which is also rich in nutrients. During the summer they are abundant here, having returned to warmer waters for the season. The oiliness of mackerel means that it pairs really nicely with strong flavours; gooseberries were an obvious choice for me as their season coincides with the return of the mackerel. It's almost like nature wants us to eat them together. This horseradish dressing is punchy but balances the plate really well. A lovely barbecue fish supper to enjoy on a hot day.

For the mackerel

4 whole mackerel, finned, gutted and gills removed

4 sprigs of dill

4 sprigs of tarragon

1 lemon, thinly sliced

Sea salt

Rapeseed oil

2 heads of gem lettuce, split in half lengthways

For the horseradish ranch dressing

350ml natural yoghurt

100ml buttermilk

3 tbsp creamed horseradish

3 tbsp juice from a tin of gherkins

2 tbsp cider vinegar

2 cloves of garlic, grated

1 small bunch of dill, finely chopped

For the gooseberry salsa

200g gooseberries, thickly sliced

200g cucumber, deseeded and thickly sliced

12 mint leaves, shredded

1 tbsp cider vinegar

30g caster sugar

Make the dressing and salsa first, so everything is ready to go once the mackerel is on the barbecue. Place all the ingredients for the ranch dressing into a mixing bowl and whisk thoroughly until combined, seasoning to taste with sea salt. Store in the fridge until needed. Put all the ingredients for the salsa into a mixing bowl. Stir well, then cover and leave to macerate for 1 hour before serving.

Get the barbecue lit and wait until the coals are hot and glowing white, with no flames. Open the cavity of the mackerel and season with salt inside, then stuff each fish evenly with the dill, tarragon and lemon slices. Season the fish all over with salt and rub with rapeseed oil.

Oil and season the gem lettuces too, then place them cut side down on the barbecue along with the mackerel. Cook without moving them for 2-3 minutes, then turn the fish over and repeat.

Serve the barbecued mackerel as soon as it's cooked alongside the barbecued gem lettuce, gooseberry salsa, and a good few dollops of horseradish dressing.

CHARCOAL ROAST OCTOPUS, NDUJA BUTTER, CHIMICHURRI

SERVES 4-8

Octopus is a rare treat and once mastered, easily enjoyed. I've created this recipe to achieve the flavour we get at the pub by finishing the octopus in the charcoal oven, however you can easily convert the roasting times to a regular oven set to 220°c. Nduja, a soft Italian sausage, adds smokiness and the chimichurri dressing has a sweet flavour which complements them both so well. A real barbecue showstopper.

For brining and boiling

4 litres water
400g caster sugar
600g salt
6 bay leaves
6 juniper berries
12 black peppercorns
1 octopus
1 bulb of garlic, split in half

For the nduja butter

300g unsalted butter
4 shallots, finely diced
4 cloves of garlic, thinly sliced
50ml sherry vinegar
300g nduja sausage

For the chimichurri

200ml extra virgin olive oil
30ml red wine vinegar
50g curly parsley, chopped
20g fresh coriander, chopped
10g oregano leaves, chopped
10g fresh mint, chopped
4 cloves of garlic, finely grated
3 red chillies, deseeded and finely chopped
1 lime, zested and juiced
Sea salt

First, make the brine for the octopus. In a suitable saucepan, combine the water, sugar and salt, then add 4 of the bay leaves with the juniper berries and peppercorns. Bring to the boil, stirring occasionally. Remove from the heat once all the sugar has dissolved. Set aside to cool to room temperature, then fully submerge the octopus in the brine for 1 hour. Remove, rinse thoroughly with cold water, and pat dry.

Set a large pan of water on the hob, drop in the halved garlic bulb and remaining 2 bay leaves, then bring to a rapid boil. Place the brined octopus into the boiling water, bring to the boil once more and then reduce to a medium simmer. Cover and allow to cook for 45 minutes.

Remove the pan from the hob and let the octopus cool in the water, uncovered. When cool, remove from the pan and slice up the connecting tissue between each tentacle with a sharp knife, allowing you to cut them off as close to the beak as possible. Once all the tentacles are removed, store them in the fridge until needed.

Now make the nduja butter. Place a large frying pan on a medium heat and add 50g of the butter. Once melted, add the shallots and cook on a medium heat until golden, then add the garlic and cook for a further 2 minutes. Next, add the sherry vinegar. Turn up the heat and allow this to boil away to a syrupy consistency. Now add the nduja, breaking it up with a wooden spoon as you stir. Cook the nduja for 5 minutes, then add the remaining butter, stirring constantly to combine everything as it cooks. Set aside in a container, stirring as it cools to ensure the nduja is distributed evenly.

For the chimichurri, place all the ingredients except the chillies into a food processor and carefully pulse to a coarse paste. Once completed, stir in the finely chopped chilli and season to taste with salt.

On a hot barbecue, brush the prepared octopus tentacles with a little vegetable oil and cook over the fire for 10 minutes, turning halfway through. Using a fire-safe pan, reheat the nduja butter on the barbecue. Plate the tentacles, generously glazing them with the butter, then drizzle over the chimichurri to serve.

SMOKED HADDOCK & SWEETCORN CHOWDER WITH SOFT BOILED EGGS

SERVES 4

This is a recipe that forever evokes a powerful sense of place in my mind, taking me all the way back to childhood holidays in Dungeness. There is a beauty in the bleakness of Dungeness, Britain's only desert. Even on scorching summer days, there is a hindering wind that whips its way along the exposed shingle. Despite this, there is nowhere I'd rather be sat to enjoy a bowl of this smoked haddock chowder. The smell of the sea mingling with the distant whistle chimes of the light railway and occasional hint of coal smoke as they thunder past, the world around me suddenly encapsulated in the bowl in front of me... That is true peace.

50g unsalted butter

2 leeks, white parts finely sliced

2 cloves of garlic, grated

2 potatoes, peeled and finely diced

400ml fish or vegetable stock

200ml whole milk

200ml double cream

4 eggs

600g smoked haddock fillets, skinned, boned, and cut into 4cm pieces

400g sweetcorn kernels

Sea salt

Black pepper

1 small bunch of dill, leaves picked

1 small bunch of chervil, leaves picked

In a large saucepan, melt the butter over a medium heat. Add the sliced leeks and sauté until they turn translucent, then add the garlic and cook for a further 2 minutes. Add the diced potatoes to the pot and cook for a few minutes, stirring occasionally to avoid them sticking.

Pour in the stock, followed by the milk and cream. Stir well to combine. Bring the mixture to a gentle simmer and let it cook for about 10 minutes or until the potatoes are tender.

Meanwhile, bring a separate pan of water to the boil. Gently lower the eggs into the boiling water and cook for 6 minutes for soft-boiled eggs. When the time is up, transfer the eggs immediately to a bowl of iced water. Once cool, carefully peel the eggs and set aside in the fridge until needed.

Add the smoked haddock and sweetcorn to the chowder. Stir gently and let it simmer for another 5 minutes or until the haddock flakes easily. Season to taste with salt and a generous twist of black pepper.

To serve, ladle the chowder into bowls. Cut the soft-boiled eggs in half and place them on top of the chowder, allowing 2 minutes for them to warm through. Finish with the fresh herb leaves.

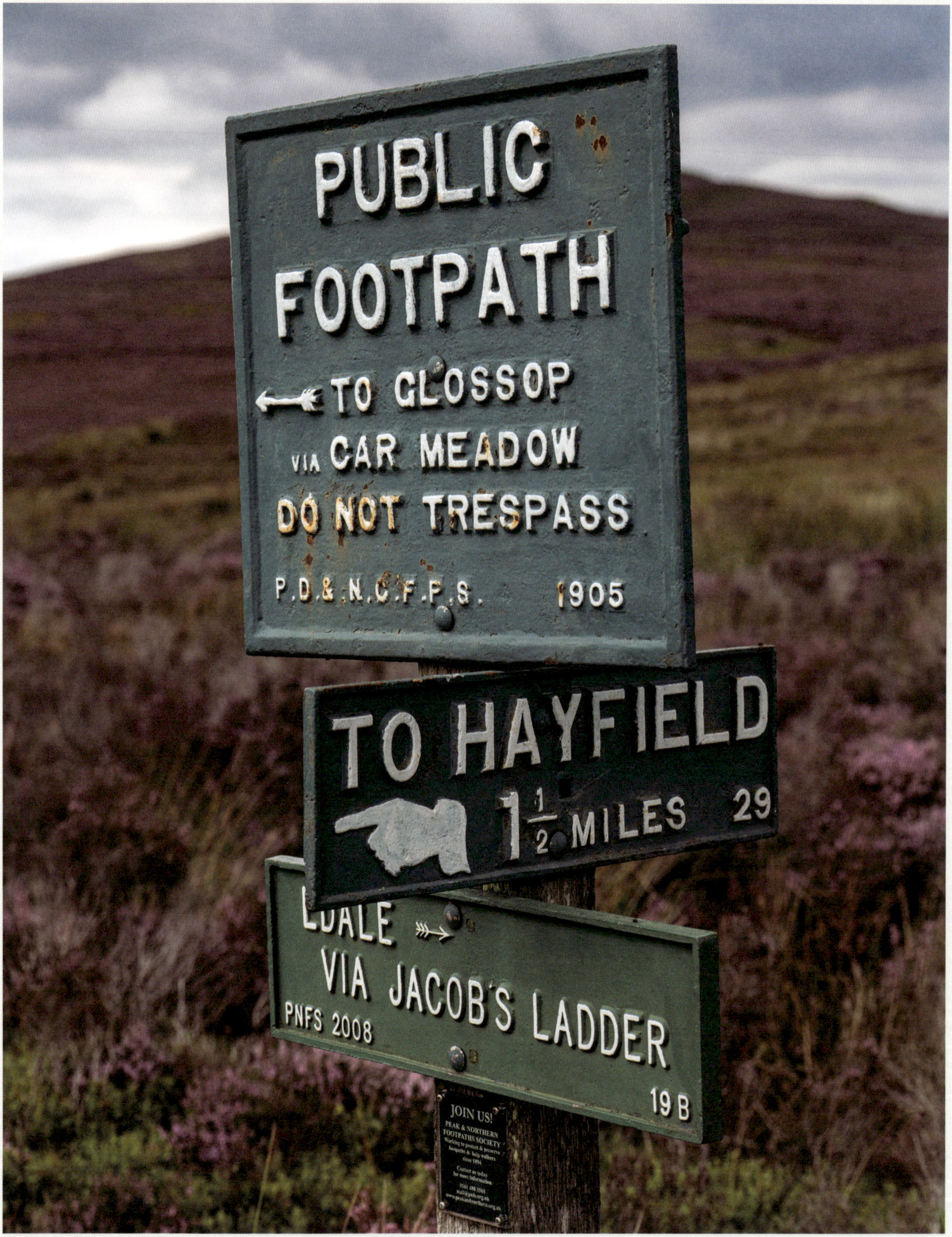

PUBLIC FOOTPATH

← TO GLOSSOP
VIA CAR MEADOW
DO NOT TRESPASS

P.D.& N.C.F.P.S.   1905

TO HAYFIELD
☞ 1½ MILES   29

…DALE ➢
VIA JACOB'S LADDER

PNFS 2008

19 B

JOIN US!
PEAK & NORTHERN
FOOTPATHS SOCIETY

SEA TROUT, SAMPHIRE, FENNEL, BUTTER BEAN & TOMATO BROTH

SERVES 6

Early July sees an influx of sea trout into our rivers as they return to their spawning grounds for the summer. We celebrate their return by only ordering a few fish every year, allowing people to taste a beautiful, seasonal, and native fish without putting unnecessary pressure on their stocks. It is of equal importance to me that our guests understand that this is a delicious yet precious fish that needs our help to have a sustainable future. Like salmon, these muscular fish have a delicate flavour and texture and therefore don't need punchy flavours to make them worthwhile. This summer broth is so light and fresh, I could have a bowl just on its own.

Sea salt

Rapeseed oil

1 litre fish stock

750ml vegetable stock

180g cherry tomatoes, halved

6 x 170g sea trout portions

50g unsalted butter

120g samphire

120g fennel, thinly sliced

240g cooked butter beans, rinsed

1 bunch of curly parsley, finely chopped

1 bunch of chervil, finely chopped

1 bunch of dill, finely chopped

Place the fish and veg stock in a large pan and bring to the boil, then turn down to a medium heat and reduce by half, seasoning with sea salt to taste.

Lay the cherry tomatoes on a baking tray, season with salt and drizzle with oil, then use a cook's blowtorch to lightly char the skins until blackened. If you don't have a blowtorch, place them in a preheated oven at 250°c for 5 minutes. Set aside.

Heat a large frying pan on the hob with a little rapeseed oil. Once hot, add the sea trout portions skin side down and reduce the heat to medium. Fry on the skin side for 8 minutes without moving the fish. Just before turning, season the flesh with a little sea salt. Turn the fish over and add the butter. Once the butter is fully melted and foaming, take the pan off the heat but leave the fish in the pan for 2-3 minutes, then remove and pat dry with a little kitchen roll.

5 minutes before serving the dish, add the blackened tomatoes, samphire, fennel, butter beans and herbs to the broth. Cover with a lid and cook for 5 minutes, then taste to check the seasoning.

Serve the broth in deep bowls with the sea trout on top.

SOLE GRENOBLOISE

SERVES 4

There's something so deeply satisfying about cooking fish on the bone. A whole flat fish is the best example of that. The bone retains moisture in the flesh, which is easily scraped off the skeleton once cooked thanks to it running parallel to the plate. Sole Grenobloise, a traditional French dish, celebrates the simplicity of classic fish cookery and everything that goes so well with fish. It is simultaneously light and wholesome, and intensely rewarding. Served with buttered summer greens and a glass of Chablis, sitting outside enjoying the birdsong at Golden Hour, this is true perfection and happiness for me.

250g unsalted butter, softened

1 clove of garlic, finely grated

1 tsp Dijon mustard

½ lemon, juiced

¼ tsp cayenne pepper

Sea salt

4 whole flat fish, scaled and cleaned (400g each, preferably lemon sole, dover sole, megrim or plaice)

Vegetable oil

2 shallots, finely diced

2 gherkins, finely diced

2 tbsp lilliput capers

1 tbsp chopped dill

1 tbsp chopped curly parsley

1 tbsp chopped chervil

½ lemon, cut into segments

40 croutons

Mix the softened butter with the grated garlic, Dijon mustard, lemon juice, cayenne, and a pinch of salt. Heat a pan on the hob and melt the butter gently at first.

Preheat a grill to its highest setting. Pat the fish dry and place on the grill tray, season with salt and lightly cover with oil. Place under the grill for 5 minutes, then flip over and cook for a further 4 minutes. Transfer the sole to warm plates ready to serve, giving them time to rest. If the fish have yielded any juices to the grill tray, add them to the hot butter.

Turn the heat up under the pan on the hob and get the butter just to the point of foaming, then add the shallots, gherkins, capers, dill, and parsley. Remove from the heat immediately but continue to stir for a minute.

Pour the hot butter sauce over the rested fish, then finish with the chopped chervil, lemon segments and croutons.

ROAST NOISETTE OF LAMB, COCKLES, SAMPHIRE, SALSA VERDE

SERVES 6

This is a fantastic summer dish, making the most of salty marsh samphire at the height of its season. These sea flavours pair so well with herbaceous, earthy lamb, and a punchy, fresh salsa verde lifts the entire dish to a whole different level. I've chosen a noisette of lamb for this, which is a boneless cut from the saddle. It provides gorgeous lean lamb meat rolled in a thick protective layer of fat which helps retain moisture and flavour. All good butchers will be able to prepare a lamb noisette for you.

1kg lamb noisette, rolled and tied

2 shallots, finely diced

500g cockles in the shell

300g samphire

125ml white wine

50g unsalted butter

For the salsa verde

4 cloves of garlic, peeled

12 salted anchovy fillets

2 tbsp lilliput capers

2 large gherkins

40g flat leaf parsley leaves

40g mint leaves

30g dill, stalks removed

30g blue nasturtium leaves or rocket

2 tbsp wholegrain mustard

2 tbsp red wine vinegar

150ml rapeseed oil

Sea salt

You can make the salsa verde in advance. Place all the ingredients in a food processor and blitz to form a thick green paste. Season to taste with sea salt, then set aside in the fridge until serving.

Preheat your oven to 200°c. Place a large frying on a high heat. Once hot, add the lamb noisette fat side down and sear all over for 2-3 minutes, basting it in the rendered fat as you go. Keep searing until the fat has rendered to a golden-brown colour, then transfer to a roasting tin and bake for 8-20 minutes depending on how pink you like your lamb. If you have a meat thermometer, 46°c is perfect for medium rare. Once done, leave the lamb to rest for the same amount of time it was in the oven.

Meanwhile, heat a little rapeseed oil in a saucepan and gently sweat the shallots on a medium heat until golden. Add the cockles, samphire and wine, bring to the boil, cover with a lid and cook for 4-6 minutes or until the cockle shells have popped open. Discard any that haven't opened by this point.

Stir in the unsalted butter to help thicken the pan juices, then pour the cockle mixture onto a platter. Slice the rested lamb noisette and place on top of the platter, then finish with spoonfuls of the salsa verde. Serve with buttered new potatoes and a crisp salad for a larger feast.

TRADITIONAL ROAST GROUSE, DAMSON SAUCE

SERVES 4

We're very fortunate here to be surrounded by stunning heather moorland, which in turn means we have access to some of England's finest red grouse. This intensely flavoured game bird is the first permitted to be shot in the season. We buy grouse sparingly, enjoying this local and delicious animal over a few short weeks with an in-house cap on how many we buy. The ethics of shooting game is complex, and it is up to us to sustainably manage the habitats of these incredible creatures to be able to enjoy them. This is a foolproof way for cooking grouse at home, paired with in-season damsons to cut through the intensity of the game flavour.

4 oven-ready grouse, plus necks and giblets
8 rashers of smoked streaky bacon
1 bunch of heather
Unsalted butter
Rapeseed oil
Sea salt

For the sauce
1 onion, roughly chopped
1 carrot, roughly chopped
1 stick of celery, roughly chopped
1 bay leaf
1 clove of garlic, crushed
175ml red wine
400ml water
100g whole damsons
25ml red wine vinegar
10g cornflour

Start the sauce first by placing the grouse necks and giblets into a saucepan with the onion, carrot, celery, bay leaf and a splash of rapeseed oil. Fry on a medium heat for 6-7 minutes until golden brown.

Add the garlic clove and red wine to the saucepan, bring to the boil and reduce the volume of liquid by half. Add the water, bring back to the boil and reduce by a third, then strain the liquid through a fine sieve into a clean pan. Add the damsons and bring to the boil once more. Once the damsons have broken down into the sauce, strain it again to remove the stones and then scoop half of the damson flesh back into the sauce. Set aside to finish later.

Preheat your oven to 220°c. Season the grouse all over with oil and salt, including the cavities. Lay two rashers of bacon over the breasts of each bird and top with a large knob of unsalted butter. Insert a sprig of heather into each cavity and place in a roasting tin. Roast in the oven for 8 minutes, then remove the bacon. Place the birds back in the oven for a further 12 minutes. Remove from the roasting tin and allow to rest for 10 minutes before carving.

Meanwhile, finish the sauce. Place the empty roasting tin on the hob and heat gently, then add the red wine vinegar to deglaze it: bring to the boil and scrape the tin as you go to extract the flavour. Pour the damson sauce into the tin and bring to the boil. Mix the cornflour with a little water to make a paste, then whisk this into the sauce to thicken it. Adjust the seasoning to taste, then serve with the rested and carved grouse.

HARISSA ROAST CARROTS, PICKLED CARROTS, SPLIT PEA PURÉE, CARROT TOP DRESSING, DUKKA

SERVES 4

Vegan dishes always present a unique challenge to kitchens as we have to change our approach to achieving balance; protein is so easily managed normally as we have meat, fish, dairy, and eggs to rely on. I've packed it into this African-inspired dish through split peas and a lovely fragrant dukka, loaded with seeds and nuts. This is always a big hit for us in the summer and is also a great way of using up those often discarded carrot tops. Their unique, peppery flavour makes them a prized possession in our kitchens with the arrival of the first bunches of English carrots.

For the carrots

2kg mixed colour heritage carrots, peeled and quartered

300ml pickling liquor (see page 249)

2 tbsp rose harissa

Sea salt

Rapeseed oil

For the dukka

50g sesame seeds

30g blanched hazelnuts

15g each coriander seeds, cumin seeds & fennel seeds

10g pumpkin seeds

10g sunflower seeds

For the split pea purée

400g yellow split peas

1 onion, finely chopped

4 cloves of garlic, finely chopped

1 bay leaf & 1 lemon, juiced

60ml extra virgin olive oil

For the dressing

100g carrot tops, leaves only

50g curly parsley leaves & 50g mint leaves

1 clove of garlic, peeled

½ tsp wholegrain mustard

½ tsp apple cider vinegar

200ml rapeseed oil

The day before you want to serve this dish, place 250g of the carrots into the pickling liquor and store in an airtight container until needed.

Preheat your oven to 160°c. Place all the ingredients for the dukka onto a baking tray with a generous pinch of sea salt, then roast for 6 minutes until aromatic. Leave to cool before gently pulsing the dukka in a food processor until it has a coarse texture, then set aside.

Place all the ingredients for the split pea purée except the oil in a pan, cover with water and bring to the boil. Reduce to a medium simmer and cook until the split peas are breaking down and soft to the touch, adding more water during this process if necessary. Once the peas are broken down and thickening to a paste-like consistency, add the olive oil and blitz with a stick blender until smooth, then season to taste and reheat when needed. Turn the oven temperature up to 190°c.

Put all the ingredients for the dressing into a food processor and blitz until smooth, then adjust the seasoning where necessary. You can add more oil if you'd like a looser dressing. Set aside.

Line a roasting tray with the remaining carrots and season with salt, then add the harissa and give them a good toss to ensure they're all thoroughly coated. Place in the hot oven for 30 minutes to roast, then serve atop the warm split pea purée with a few pickled carrots per person. Finish with the dressing and dukka to taste.

HERB ROAST CHICKEN

SERVES 4

We rarely serve chicken at the pub, purely because I believe it's always better done at home. There's something deeply satisfying and immensely rewarding about roasting a whole chicken. It may be my favourite roast to cook at home for its simplicity and the sense of comfort it brings. This will serve four on the day but will continue to give generously for two people throughout the next day as a soup base or sandwich filling, or even delicious, jellied scraps straight from the roasting tin on toast.

1 whole 2kg free-range chicken
125g unsalted butter, softened
1 bunch of curly parsley
1 bunch of chervil
1 sprig of tarragon, leaves only
2 sprigs of thyme, leaves only
1 sprig of rosemary, leaves only
4 cloves of garlic
1 lemon, zested
Sea salt and black pepper
125ml white wine

Preheat your oven to 210°c. Remove any trussing from the chicken, spread the legs wide to open the cavity and place in the centre of a roasting tin.

Place the softened butter in a mixing bowl. Roughly chop the parsley, chervil, and tarragon leaves, then add them to the butter along with the thyme and rosemary leaves. Finely grate the garlic cloves on top, then add the lemon zest, a generous pinch of salt, and a twist of black pepper. Mix everything together until evenly combined.

Spread the flavoured butter all over the chicken, inside and outside. Place the chicken in the oven for 20 minutes, then remove and baste thoroughly. Turn the oven down to 170°c. Once basted, pour the wine into the roasting tin – don't pour it over the bird.

Place the chicken back into the oven for 35 minutes. When the timer goes off, turn the oven off and open the door, but leave the bird in the oven for a further 20 minutes. This finishes the chicken beautifully, allowing it to gently finish cooking and relax in the last moments of heat before serving.

You can carve this traditionally, but I prefer this as a summer roast dinner which therefore requires no heavy gravy. Simply pull all the meat from the bones and lay it back into the roasting tin with the buttery herby juices. Serve at the table with a serving spoon.

FISH PIE

SERVES 6

I don't mean to brag, but this fish pie is so good that it has influenced people to move to Hayfield, who have since gone on to briefly work with us and are now good friends. The thing I love most about this dish is its simplicity, and using all the fish poaching liquor which takes the flavour up a few notches. It's all about the fish; no distractions of peas or hard-boiled eggs here.

For the filling

2 litres whole milk

1 onion, peeled and halved

1 bulb of garlic, cut in half

1 bay leaf

Sea salt

600g smoked haddock fillet, skinned and pin boned

200g cod fillet, skinned and pin boned

200g trout fillet, skinned and pin boned

200g raw king prawns, peeled and deveined

1 bunch of dill, finely chopped

1 lemon, zested and juiced

100g unsalted butter

100g plain flour

For the topping

1.5kg Rooster or Maris Piper potatoes, washed

150g unsalted butter

50ml double cream

2 egg yolks

Sea salt

For the filling

Preheat your oven to 180°c. Pour the milk into a large pan with the halved onion, garlic bulb, bay leaf, and a touch of salt in. Bring to a simmer and place the haddock, cod and trout into the pan. Cover and cook for around 10 minutes, then add the prawns and cook for a further 6 minutes.

Remove all the fish and prawns from the poaching pan with a slotted spoon and place into a mixing bowl. When cool enough to handle, break the fish into flakes and gently combine it with the chopped dill, lemon juice and lemon zest. Retain a litre of the warm milk, discarding the onion, garlic and bay.

In another saucepan, melt the butter. Add the flour and stir to combine, allowing the paste to cook out for 2-3 minutes. Gradually add the reserved warm milk, stirring continuously as you go, and cook until the mixture starts to thicken. Once your sauce is the right consistency, pour it over the flaked fish, using just enough to coat it all evenly. Spoon the filling into an ovenproof dish.

For the topping

While you make the filling, place the potatoes in a roasting tin and bake in the preheated oven for 45 minutes, until the flesh feels soft. Once cool enough to handle, cut each potato in half and spoon out the flesh. Heat the butter and cream in a large saucepan, then pass the potato flesh through a sieve or potato ricer into the pan. Fold in the egg yolks and season to taste with sea salt. Spoon the potato mixture into a piping bag and pipe over the filling.

Place the fish pie in the preheated oven for 40 minutes to cook, then remove and serve with greens of your choice.

CÔTE DU BOEUF, PEPPERCORN SAUCE

SERVES 2

There is something quite primal about roasting a large piece of beef over fire. An intrinsic link to our ancestors, a sense of connection between man, beast and Earth. Côte du boeuf – a thick cut ribeye steak still on the rib bone – is my favourite steak to cook. It has a higher fat content than fillet and sirloin which gives it a more robust flavour, but also a more challenging texture. Rendering the fat is key as the meat will just melt away in your mouth when done right. A classic peppercorn sauce alongside is just a perfect match.

Rapeseed oil
1 banana shallot, finely diced
50g butter
50ml brandy
500ml beef stock
100ml double cream
1 tsp English mustard
30g green peppercorns
Sea salt and black pepper
1 x 850g côte du boeuf

Make the peppercorn sauce in advance and reheat it when ready. Heat a large saucepan and add some oil. Once hot, add the shallot and half the butter to sweat on a low heat until translucent. Add the brandy and bring to the boil, reducing the volume of liquid by half.

Add the beef stock to the saucepan and reduce it by two thirds, then stir in the double cream and allow to simmer for 15 minutes. Whisk in the mustard, remaining butter, and green peppercorns, plus a twist of black pepper and a pinch of salt. Cook for a further 5 minutes, then season to taste and set aside for later.

Light your barbecue and get it raging hot, until the coals are a searing white colour. An hour before serving, remove the steak from the fridge and pat dry. Season liberally with sea salt 5 minutes before cooking. Place the steak on the barbecue and allow a crust to develop on the beef for 3-4 minutes, then flip and repeat. Now cook the steak to your liking: another 6-8 minutes each side for medium rare, and double that time for well done. If you have a meat thermometer, aim for the following internal temperatures: 42°c for rare, 50°c for medium rare, 55°c for medium.

Once cooked to your liking, allow the steak to rest for the same amount of time it took to cook. Serve alongside the reheated peppercorn sauce with a fresh salad and chunky chips.

STRAWBERRIES, TARRAGON ICE CREAM, MERINGUE, VERJUS SYRUP

SERVES 6

Another hero ingredient which has come to define the British food calendar; I would argue that most people know that the great British strawberry season coincides with the Wimbledon tennis tournament. I have vivid memories of my Grandmother Priscilla taking me to pick my own strawberries in Kent as a young boy, and I'm sure she will be quick to remind me that I ate more on our way through the fields than were in my basket at the end! Verjus is a juice made from unripened grapes, giving a sharp kick to this sweet dessert. Trust me on the tarragon ice cream; its subtle anise flavour with the strawberries is a combination you'll never forget.

750g British strawberries, quartered

For the ice cream
300ml double cream
300ml whole milk
3 egg yolks (60ml)
100g caster sugar
50g tarragon leaves, chopped

For the meringue
75g egg whites
70g caster sugar
70g icing sugar

For the syrup
375ml verjus
100g caster sugar

For the ice cream

Make this a day before serving the dessert. Pour the cream and milk into a pan and bring to the boil. Meanwhile, beat the egg yolks and sugar together in a mixing bowl. Pour the boiling cream into the bowl while whisking continuously. Once combined, pour the mixture back into the pan and cook to precisely 82°c, then pour into a suitable container with a lid. Leave to cool overnight. In the morning, pour the mix into a food processor and blitz with the tarragon, then pour it into an ice cream machine to churn. Finally, transfer the ice cream to the freezer.

For the meringue

Preheat your oven to 100°c and line a baking tray with parchment paper. In a large bowl, use a whisk or an electric mixer to beat the egg whites until stiff peaks form. Add the caster sugar and continue beating until the mixture is thick and glossy, then gently fold in the icing sugar using a spatula until well combined. Spoon the mixture into a piping bag fitted with a small round tip and pipe small drops onto the prepared baking sheet, spacing them about 2cm apart. Bake the meringue drops for about 60-90 minutes, or until they are dry and crisp, then remove from the oven and allow them to cool completely on the baking tray before transferring to an airtight container.

Place the verjus and sugar for the syrup in a small saucepan on a medium heat and reduce by a third. Allow to cool completely before serving.

Arrange the strawberries on your serving plates, dotted with the meringue drops. Top with the ice cream, and drizzle over the syrup.

GOOSEBERRY & ELDERFLOWER FOOL

SERVES 6

Just as the gooseberry bushes release their tangy green berries, the elder tree blooms with beautiful white flowers that are sweet, floral and delicious: this is nature's very own perfect flavour combination, driven by the rhythm of the seasons. Served simply here as a classic fool, this dessert will delight all who eat it in the long evenings of early summer. I've included a recipe for making your own elderflower cordial here too, for those so inclined and with 24 hours to prepare in advance.

500g gooseberries

100g caster sugar

1 lemon, zested

2 tbsp water

2 tbsp elderflower cordial

300ml double cream

100g Greek yoghurt

For the elderflower cordial (makes 2 litres)

1.5 litres water

2kg caster sugar

24 fresh elderflower heads, stalks trimmed

2 lemons, zested and sliced

75g citric acid

Rinse the gooseberries and place them in a saucepan with the caster sugar, lemon zest and water. Cook over a medium heat for 10-15 minutes until the gooseberries have softened and the mixture has thickened. Remove from the heat and stir in the elderflower cordial, then set aside to cool.

In a large mixing bowl, whisk the double cream until it forms soft peaks. Fold in the Greek yoghurt. Spoon a layer of the gooseberry mixture into 6 individual serving glasses. Top with a layer of the cream mixture, then repeat the layers until the glasses are full. Chill in the fridge for at least 1 hour before serving.

For the elderflower cordial

Put the water and sugar into a large saucepan. Gently heat without boiling until the sugar has dissolved, stirring occasionally. Once the sugar has dissolved, bring to the boil, then take off the heat.

Rinse the flowers to loosen any dirt or bugs, gently shake them dry and then transfer to the syrup along with the lemon zest, lemon slices, and citric acid. Stir well, cover the pan and leave to infuse for 24 hours.

Once infused, line a colander with muslin cloth over a large container and ladle the cordial through. Store in sterilised bottles for up to 6 weeks.

SEA BUCKTHORN POSSET, HEATHER & ALMOND BISCOTTI

SERVES 8

This recipe came about after my week at L'Enclume. They use as little citrus as possible in their quest for Britishness, and the tart sharpness of sea buckthorn is an excellent substitute. Upon returning to the pub, I changed our lemon posset to sea buckthorn which went down a treat. A great summer refresher, the recipe uses freshly pressed sea buckthorn juice. The biscotti is something of a house signature. Heather is a wonderful local ingredient that grows in abundance across the Peak District, blooming over the hills of Kinder Scout in August in a breathtaking sea of purple.

For the biscotti

200g softened butter

350g caster sugar

4 eggs

450g plain flour

2 tsp baking powder

1 tbsp dried heather flowers

½ tbsp fennel seeds

100g ground almonds

For the posset

900ml double cream

280g caster sugar

150ml sea buckthorn juice

For the biscotti

Start with the biscotti, as this can be made in advance. Preheat your oven to 170°c and line 2 baking trays with greaseproof paper.

In a large mixing bowl, beat the butter and sugar together until light and creamy. Beat in the eggs, one by one, and then fold in the flour and baking powder. Finally, add the heather flowers, fennel seeds and ground almonds. Mix thoroughly to distribute them evenly throughout the dough.

Divide the dough in half and shape into rough logs on the lined baking trays, then bake in the preheated oven for 30-35 minutes. Remove from the oven and leave to cool for 15 minutes, then cut into 5mm thick slices. Lay these slices onto the trays and toast in the oven for a further 6 minutes, then remove and leave to cool completely before storing in an airtight container.

For the posset

Put the cream and sugar in a pan and bring to the boil, stirring to dissolve the sugar. Turn the heat down to a simmer and stir for 1-2 minutes until the bubbles are quite large.

Slowly pour in the sea buckthorn juice, stirring continuously, then simmer for a further 2 minutes. Remove from the heat and skim off the layer of foam that will have formed on top of the mixture.

Pour the mixture evenly into 8 ramekins and leave to cool completely before placing in the fridge to set overnight. The following day, remove the possets from the fridge just prior to serving them alongside the biscotti.

CHOCOLATE FONDANT, BLACKCURRANT RIPPLE ICE CREAM

SERVES 6

This was the dessert which toppled our chocolate delice from the menu. It comes from the mind of our sous chef, Pedro, who had wanted to do a fondant since joining us. When we had a sudden burst of blackcurrants from our neighbour's garden one summer, everything just fell into place. Summer is the gift that keeps on giving when it comes to great British fruit and they all make a great pairing with chocolate, so feel free change up the fruit in your ripple ice cream. The perfectly melting middle of a chocolate fondant is one of life's greatest pleasures, and I hope this recipe gives you as much joy to make and eat as it does for me.

For the blackcurrant ripple ice cream

250g blackcurrants
½ lemon, juiced
150g caster sugar
200ml whole milk
300ml double cream
3 egg yolks (60ml)

For the chocolate fondants

100g unsalted butter, plus extra for greasing
100g good-quality dark chocolate
Cocoa powder, for dusting
2 eggs
2 egg yolks
100g caster sugar
2 tbsp coffee liqueur
80g plain flour

For the blackcurrant ripple ice cream

Make the ice cream the day before serving this dessert. First, you'll need to make a blackcurrant compote. Place the blackcurrants, lemon juice and 50g of the sugar into a saucepan. Gently heat until the fruit begins to break down and gets a little sticky, then leave to cool in the fridge.

Place the milk and cream into a saucepan and bring to the boil. In a mixing bowl, beat the egg yolks with the remaining 100g of sugar. Pour the boiling cream into the bowl, whisking continuously to combine.

Place the ice cream mix back into the saucepan and cook to precisely 82°c, then pour into a suitable container with a lid. Leave to cool overnight, then churn in the ice cream machine first thing in the morning. While still a little soft, fold in the blackcurrant compote, then transfer to the freezer.

For the chocolate fondants

Preheat your oven to 160°c. Lightly grease six ramekins with a little unsalted butter and then liberally sprinkle with cocoa powder. Place in the fridge while you prepare the fondant mixture. Bring a pan of water to the boil and place a mixing bowl over it with the butter and chocolate in. Melt while stirring continuously and then remove from the heat, stirring until smooth.

In a separate bowl, whisk the eggs, egg yolks and sugar together until pale and thickening. Fold in the melted chocolate mixture, followed by the liqueur and flour. Stir thoroughly to remove any lumps.

Divide the mixture evenly between the prepared ramekins and bake in the preheated oven for 12 minutes. Once done, carefully turn out the chocolate fondants onto warm plates, using a knife to run around the edges and loosen them. Serve immediately, with a dollop of the ice cream on the side.

MEET THE SUPPLIERS

Our suppliers are the backbone of our business. We seek out the very best of British produce available to us and, wherever possible, as locally as we can. The rolling hills of the Peak District provide some of the finest outdoor grazing space in the country for cattle and sheep, and we are incredibly lucky to have a world class butcher with their own co-located abattoir just four miles from the pub. It puts us in the privileged position of working with the finest local meat and championing its locality on our menu. The High Peak lamb in particular is a phenomenal product with its own unique taste that can only be found around here.

There are challenges associated with our location too; the Peak District is not renowned for its vegetable growing, and we are completely landlocked. Through our friends at Organic North, who are based in Manchester, we have access to seasonal produce selected only from organically certified farms across the UK. This not only drives the direction of our menu, following the natural rhythm of the seasons, but ensures we are buying the best British produce at the right time of year. You'll never see asparagus on our menu outside of April to June, strawberries appear only in the summer, and hardy root vegetables only in the winter. For me, this is a key indicator of quality and shows how much we care about what we do. Buying organic produce also supports traditional farming practices vital for a sustainable future, which we should be at the forefront of promoting.

Our fish is predominantly sourced from ports in Scotland, with Shetland and Peterhead providing the best selection of North Sea fish throughout the year. Much like vegetables, fish are also seasonal, driven by ocean temperatures and spawning seasons. Beautiful cod in the winter, no mussels in summer but plenty of incredible shellfish in the Autumn: the rhythm of the world around us continues to dictate what we serve and when.

If you're interested in learning more about the produce we use and where it comes from, a few of our key suppliers have shared some insights here, in their own words.

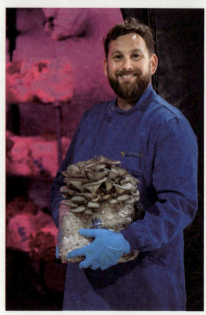

Mettrick's Butchers

"More people are wanting to know more about where their food comes from and, most importantly, where their meat comes from. Here at Mettrick's we source our meat from farms within the Peak District, the northwest and the midlands, with some slight seasonal variation. All the cattle, pigs and lambs passing through our small abattoir in Glossop will have travelled only a short distance before arriving with us. This is important to us, not only for animal welfare reasons, but because we pride ourselves on being able to answer any query about the provenance of all our meat. We believe this is something only a handful of butchers in the UK today can honestly claim to be able to do. Our customers often ask where their chosen cuts of meat came from, and all our staff have the knowledge to answer those questions thoroughly.

We don't cut corners to save a few pence, nor are we trying to compete with well-known supermarket chains that process meat on a much larger but far less transparent scale. We are more concerned with the quality of our meat, its freshness, its taste and its journey to us. This ethos has led us to win a multitude of awards over the years, including Britain's Best Butcher, Britain's Top Shop National Winner, and Best Online Butcher. John Mettrick himself has been awarded the title Master Butcher, one of only ten people to receive this accolade in the UK. You may have seen us featured on TV too, alongside The Hairy Bikers and on Ready Steady Cook, Saturday Kitchen, Countryfile, and The One Show among others.

JW Mettrick & Son Butchers has been in the Mettrick family for more than a century, passed down through five generations. Our speciality is sourcing the best quality meat from local farms with whom we have longstanding relationships. The meat is dry-aged to create the best flavour and then carefully butchered to very high specifications. We enjoy identifying shopping trends through our customers which challenges us to innovate so we can sell the whole carcass of our animals. We especially enjoy working with Luke and his team because they believe in the same ethos of quality local meat, sustainably sourced, treated with care and respect. The excellent cooking and presentation of the meat we supply them with is a compliment to our business and we are very proud to be associated with The Pack Horse."

The Mushroom Emporium

"We grow a wide variety of gourmet and medicinal mushrooms for local chefs, delivered within minutes of harvesting them on our small farm in the glorious Peak District. We also create 'grow your own from home kits' called The Fungi FarmBox, plus other mycology and mushroom related products. My father Ian came up with The Mushroom Emporium concept and has been helping me every step of the way. He taught me the proper techniques and skills to cultivate and grow the finest gourmet mushrooms the world has to offer. The Mushroom Emporium is receiving a lot of praise and producing unrivalled produce which makes us both very happy!

From start to finish, mushroom farming is so varied and interesting that there's never a dull moment. Testing our mushrooms in dishes created by the chefs who use our produce is definitely a highlight! The Pack Horse develops menus that make your mouth water just by looking at them. Luke is a great advocate for local produce and even takes the time to visit small independent producers like us, learning all about where his ingredients come from and how they are prepared. He only uses the best local produce available, which we are proud to provide The Pack Horse with."

Robin, mycologist and farmer, The Mushroom Emporium

Organic North

"We're a Manchester-based, member-run wholesalers committed exclusively to organic produce. We run on a unique zero-waste model that eliminates food waste at a point in the supply chain that traditionally creates a lot of it. We've been trading since 1997 and we're on a mission to help redefine the UK food scene. We look to buy fruit and veg for taste over yield or weight and buy as locally as we can too. We support over 100 independent growers and suppliers, many of whom are customers of ours too. Having so many cyclical relationships with our suppliers and sharing so many missions and values with them is one of the true joys of our job.

We're passionate about making the best veg that's out there as accessible to the most people possible. For far too long, organic produce has been the preserve of the privileged in the UK and we're on a mission to change that. As we grow, we look to plug all the gaps in the season we have, support more growers, and help turn more farmers over to a more sustainable way of producing food than the intensive, high-input methods that have come to dominate our domestic food systems.

It's always a pleasure to work with establishments like The Pack Horse who are so clearly interested in the quality and provenance of their produce. It's more enjoyable still when they've the craft and imagination to be able to make that produce front and centre on their menus. It will always be a joy to work with folk who have such reverence for the food that they cook with."

Autumn

Autumn greets us like an old friend every year. There is a sombre quality to its arrival: the waning of the year playing out in front of us, as all that was once youthful and green withers away. The days develop a crispness, and as the sun lowers in the sky the world is filtered into sepia. Dramatic hues of yellows, reds and browns sweep across the landscape in gradual strokes, as if an artist has spilled their paints on a watercolour canvas. Yet Autumn continues to provide in stunning fashion, gifted like pockets of wisdom from a life fulfilled.

Summer berry sweetness and acidity is replaced by autumnal stone fruit, ripe from a hot summer with honeyed, almost tropical flavours. There is a natural complexity here, alluding to Autumn's great understanding. Green courgettes are swiftly replaced with rotund and textured squashes displaying every shade of the season among their varieties. Our world-famous orchards bring the first apples of the year, and this is prime time for alliums and root vegetables too, fattening under soil in the summer rains, ripe for the picking on a dry autumnal morning. Just when you think there is tragedy in the falling leaves, wild mushrooms erupt from the earth as a tonic to all the summer sweetness. It is a plentiful time, a beautiful time, etched with the sorrow of our dear friend Autumn giving us so much when it knows its days are numbered.

In the kitchen, Autumn is a joyous time. For British produce this is undoubtedly the most abundance we get to work with, and as we move into cooler days, so the food becomes more warming. Game season is in full swing, and such rich flavours are beautifully balanced by sweet root vegetables and hearty kale. The colours of Autumn are also transposed onto our plates with squashes left unadulterated where possible, heavier brown sauces brought back into play, and gamey red meat with mushrooms bringing earthiness to our plates. When caught in the delicious light of golden hour, sat in the front window of the pub, Autumn manifests itself across every sense.

The teeming Autumn, big with rich increase,
Bearing the wanton burden of the prime,
Like widow'd wombs after their lords' decease.

From Sonnet 97, William Shakespeare

OUR SEASONAL HIGHLIGHTS

SEPTEMBER	OCTOBER	NOVEMBER
Blackberries	Apples	Red cabbage
Squash	Wild mushrooms	Parsnips
Plums	Leeks	Kale
Runner beans	Beetroot	Chestnuts

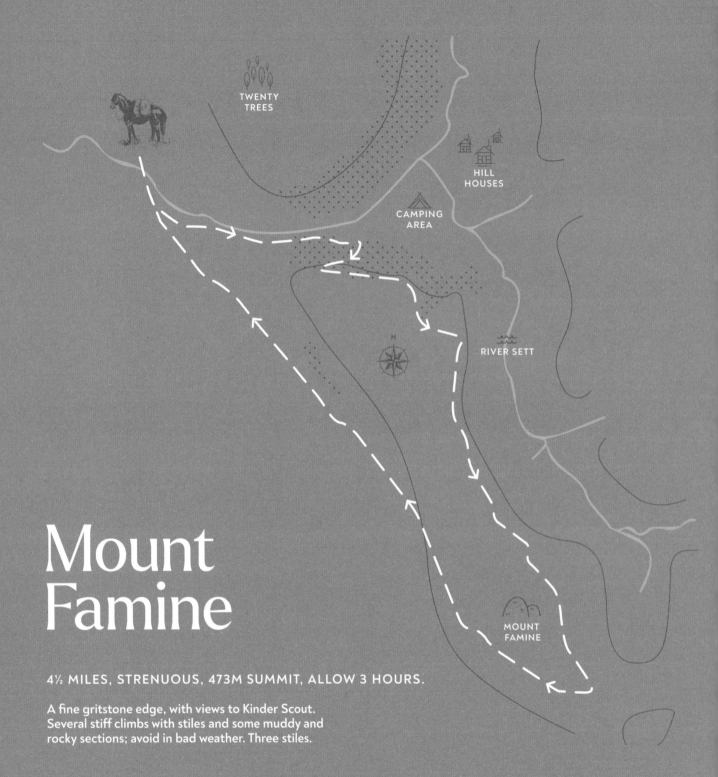

Mount Famine

4½ MILES, STRENUOUS, 473M SUMMIT, ALLOW 3 HOURS.

A fine gritstone edge, with views to Kinder Scout. Several stiff climbs with stiles and some muddy and rocky sections; avoid in bad weather. Three stiles.

Mount Famine contains the site of an early Bronze Age burial mound, providing evidence of human existence here from 5,000 years ago. Some pottery has been excavated from the site, suggesting it may have been used often for other rituals from several nearby settlements. The view from the summit overlooking Kinder Scout is quite breathtaking. Enclosure Acts which were passed between 1750 and 1850 resulted in land such as commons and moorlands being allocated to private landowners. These landowners walled off parts of their new land in order to lease it to tenant farmers. Unfortunately, the land was often unsuitable for successful farming, and despite their hard work, the tenant farmers often went hungry. The struggles of these farmers are sometimes memorialised in placenames. Mount Famine is an example of this in the Dark Peak. Other notable examples include Starvation Hill, Never Gains, Famish Acre, and Mount Misery – all in Dartmoor.

From the front door of The Pack Horse, turn left. Bear right over the River Sett and keep left of the church up the main road, Church Street, passing The George Hotel and the fish and chip shop. At the top of Church Street, turn left and left again into Valley Road.

Follow Valley Road, keeping left following the river, but not crossing it. After a row of terraced houses on the right, the path descends to a no-through road. Keep left again at the fork bearing the owl carving, keeping the high stone retaining wall on your right. Descend to the river and after the last houses follow the riverside path, ignoring a footbridge. At a fork, turn right away from the river towards the woods to a gate and climb through woodland beyond, with a campsite to your left. Just before the trees end on the left, at a crossroads of paths, turn sharp right onto a signposted footpath that angles up through the wood. Follow the path past the giant old oak tree and traverse all the way to the top. There is a family of deer in these woods which may be visible at any point. At the top of the woodland hill turn left, staying within the trees, with a stone wall on your right. Follow this path and eventually you leave the trees but continue along the wall to meet a crossing path. Carry straight on towards a ladder stile over a crossing wall.

The path now follows the wall above the steep rough-pastured slopes of the Sett Valley, with wide views to Kinder Scout. At a bend in the wall, a fine view of the ridge ahead is revealed, and the path continues along the wall above a couple of rocky undulations before dropping to the Pennine Bridleway. Continue ahead to another ladder stile and then bear right through a gap in an old wall. After a further wall, a rough path winds steeply up towards the top of Mount Famine, which has a couple of false summits; a flatter but less well-used path bypasses the high point to the left. Once you finally reach the top marked by some jutting rocks, take in the view and cast your mind back to those Bronze Age settlers who would have seen the land much as you do today.

When ready to descend, continue ahead to a stile, then descend to meet the Pennine Bridleway. If you're feeling energetic, you can continue to the cairn at the top of South Head, returning the same way. Turn right along the Pennine Bridleway track, which gradually descends with a wall on the left and through a gate. After more gates, at a junction with another track, bear right. At a crossing of tracks, the Pennine Bridleway departs to the right, but we carry straight on. Eventually the track bends left to meet Highgate Road, but a narrow, sunken path continues ahead for a short distance before also joining the road. Follow Highgate Road downhill for three-quarters of a mile, back to the village of Hayfield. Retrace your earlier steps down Church Street and over the bridge, bearing left back to The Pack Horse.

MANCHESTER EGG

MAKES 8

Our signature bar snack, now instantly synonymous with the pub. Being so close to Manchester, I felt it was important to have a bar snack that has a true sense of location. Unlike a Scotch egg, the egg inside a Manchester egg is pickled, and then wrapped in a black pudding and sausage meat mix. The soft boiling of the egg is critical, as its runniness becomes tamed by the pickling process, giving the yolk a delicious jammy quality and a hint of brown sauce flavour.

8 medium free-range eggs
400g black pudding
400g minced pork
8g chopped sage
50g fine breadcrumbs
100g plain flour
100ml egg yolk
200g panko breadcrumbs

For the pickle
1 litre white wine
1 litre white wine vinegar
500g caster sugar
½ tsp coriander seeds
¼ tsp chilli flakes
1 allspice berry
1 clove

Place all the ingredients for the pickle into a saucepan, bring to the boil and then reduce to a simmer for 10 minutes. Set aside and leave to cool to room temperature, then pass through a sieve and place in the fridge.

Bring a large pan of water to a rolling boil. Fill a 4-litre ice cream tub with iced water. Drop all the eggs simultaneously into the boiling water and boil for 6 minutes, then immediately plunge into the iced water. Once cool throughout, carefully peel off the shell and place the eggs into your pickle. Cover with a baking parchment cartouche and leave in the fridge for 3 days.

Place the black pudding, minced pork, sage, and fine breadcrumbs into a food processor and blitz to form a smooth paste.

Remove the eggs from the pickle and pat dry. Take 100g of the black pudding mix, lightly flour and roll out to 5mm thickness. Place the mix in your hand with the pickled egg on top, then carefully encase the egg tightly in the black pudding mix, making sure all air is removed. Repeat to make 8.

Preheat a deep fat fryer to 180°c. Roll the encased eggs through the plain flour, egg yolk and then panko breadcrumbs, in that order. Deep fry the coated eggs for 7 minutes. Drain off any excess oil and slice in half to serve.

BEETROOT RISOTTO

SERVES 6

I love making risotto at home and it's one of the first things I taught myself to cook properly. They take some concentration though: 30 seconds away from the stove at the wrong moment and your rice can weld itself to your pan. This is an adaptation of a dish we featured just before Covid hit, so it sadly never got a full run on the menu. Folding in the beetroot purée is the key to an intense colour, and crapaudine beetroot is an earthy heritage variety which adds a lovely finishing touch when honey roasted. Crème fraiche really complements the intense beetroot flavour.

1 crapaudine beetroot, peeled and cut into 6 long wedges

1 tbsp rapeseed oil

1 tbsp runny honey

300ml beetroot juice

800g cooked beetroot, grated

60ml rapeseed oil

60g unsalted butter

2 shallots, finely diced

2 sprigs of thyme, leaves only

2 cloves of garlic, grated

400g arborio rice

175ml white wine

1 litre vegetable stock

75g Spenwood or parmesan, grated

1 lemon, zested

Sea salt

Crème fraiche, to serve

Preheat your oven to 170°c. Toss the crapaudine beetroot wedges in the tablespoon of oil and honey with a pinch of sea salt. Lay them on a baking tray and roast for 45 minutes until soft.

Pour the beetroot juice over the grated beetroot in a food processor and blitz until smooth. Season with a little salt and pass through a fine sieve to make a purée, then set aside for later.

Heat the oil and butter in a large saucepan over a medium heat. Add the shallots and thyme, cook over a medium heat until softened, then add the garlic and rice, stirring to coat in the butter and oil.

Turn up the heat and add the white wine. Bring to the boil and reduce until around 3 tablespoons of liquid remain. Now add the vegetable stock 200ml at a time, stirring continuously, adding the next 200ml when the first has been absorbed. Repeat until you've added all the stock and the rice has absorbed it all. This process should take around 20-25 minutes.

When the rice feels soft, add the cheese and lemon zest, then fold in the beetroot purée until the risotto turns bright purple. Season to taste with sea salt and spoon into your serving bowls, topping each one with a couple of roasted crapaudine beetroot wedges and a spoonful of crème fraiche.

AN ENGLISH AUTUMN POROTOS GRANADOS

SERVES 6

This recipe harks back to my student days when I shared a house with my mates and was falling in love with cooking. Sam and I were engrossed in River Cottage Veg at the time so when we stumbled upon Hugh Fearnley-Whittingstall's version of this classic, we had to give it a go. We hadn't been shopping but had a cupboard full of bits and a fridge of vegetables well past their best. Despite our plethora of leftovers, it impressed us so much that it became one of our household staples. This slightly refined version is great at the transition of summer to Autumn, utilising the best of both seasons for a hearty and delicious stew-come-soup.

2 tbsp rapeseed oil

1 onion, finely chopped

1 bulb of fennel, finely chopped

750g butternut, Crown Prince or onion squash, peeled, deseeded and cut into 2cm chunks

3 cloves of garlic, grated

1 tsp smoked paprika

1 tsp cumin seeds

2 tsp chopped fresh oregano

1 tsp chopped fresh marjoram

400g tinned borlotti beans, drained and rinsed

1 litre vegetable stock

1 bay leaf

200g sweetcorn kernels

200g fine green beans, cut into 2cm pieces

Sea salt and black pepper

Sourdough, to serve

Take a large saucepan and place over a medium heat on the hob, then add the oil. Once hot, gently fry the onion and fennel for about 10 minutes.

Add the squash, garlic, paprika, and cumin to the pan and cook for a further 5 minutes, stirring occasionally. Add half the oregano and marjoram, then cook for another minute.

Stir in the drained beans, stock and bay leaf. Bring to the boil, reduce to a simmer and cook until the squash is just tender. Now add the sweetcorn and green beans, then simmer for a further 5 minutes.

To finish, stir in the remaining herbs and allow the flavours to infuse for a couple of minutes. Season to taste with salt and pepper, then serve alongside thickly sliced and buttered sourdough.

SCALLOPS BAKED IN SEAWEED BUTTER, GARLIC & THYME CRUMB

SERVES 4

The sweet luxurious meat of a scallop is a real jewel of our oceans and needs very little doing to it for a fantastic meal. Baking them in the shell allows all the flavours to marry as one, and the meeting of hot butter and crispy breadcrumbs brings a childlike joy to many a guest. Source your scallops sensibly from a good local fishmonger, who will also be able to provide the shells for baking.

12 large king scallops, roe on

4 slices of stale bread

50ml extra virgin rapeseed oil

2 cloves of garlic, grated

4 sprigs of thyme, leaves only

250g unsalted butter

Maldon sea salt

1 small bunch of curly parsley

1 small bunch of chervil

1 lemon, zested and juiced

1 tbsp kombu flakes

1 tbsp smoked dulse flakes

1 shallot, finely diced

1 tbsp lilliput capers

Prep the scallops the day before. Peel away the roe and the membrane that encases the scallop; this should all come off in one go but ensure there's no membrane remaining, as it will tighten the scallop up when it cooks. Preheat your oven to 70°c and place the roe on a baking tray in the oven to cook overnight.

In the morning, remove the roes and blitz in a food processor until powdered, then set aside. Clean the processor and blitz the stale bread into breadcrumbs. Preheat your oven to 160°c.

Dress a mixing bowl with the rapeseed oil, a pinch of salt, the grated garlic and thyme leaves, then add the breadcrumbs and mix thoroughly. Spread over a baking sheet and season with a few pinches of the dehydrated scallop roe powder, then place in the oven for 10 minutes until just turning golden brown.

Melt the butter in a pan and remove from the heat once fully melted. Place the parsley, chervil, lemon zest and juice, both seaweeds and a good pinch of sea salt into a food processor. Begin to blitz on a high speed as you pour in the melted butter, blitzing until it turns green. Pour this over the diced shallot and capers, stirring to combine evenly, then season to taste.

Preheat your oven to 180°c. Place the scallops either in their shells or an ovenproof roasting dish, topped with a few spoonfuls of the seaweed butter and then the garlic and thyme crumb. Bake for 10 minutes, then remove and serve immediately.

This recipe can also be adapted for charcoal ovens or barbecues with a lid; we cook it like this at the pub for extra flavour. When the charcoal is burning bright amber, bake the scallops for 3-4 minutes.

LAMB KOFTAS, SHEEP'S MILK LABNEH, PICKLED RED ONION

SERVES 6

Given our location, it would be silly of us to not utilise the incredible lamb reared in the High Peak. This kofta recipe first appeared as a starter a few years ago and has now found a permanent home on our bar menu. Always a hit in the summer, the well-rounded spice of ras el hanout – which translates as 'top of the shop' in Arabic, hinting at the luxuriousness of the spice blend – is a perfect match for lamb. Labneh is an easy yoghurt-cheese to get to grips with, and if you have the means to barbecue the koftas, you've got yourself a great little outdoor party with this dish.

For the labneh

500ml sheep's yoghurt
1 clove of garlic, grated
1 lemon, zested
A pinch of sea salt

For the pickled onion

450ml pickling liquor (see page 249)
2 red onions, thinly sliced

For the koftas

1.5kg minced lamb
2 tbsp ras el hanout
1 tsp smoked paprika
1 tsp curry powder
1 tsp mint sauce
½ tsp garlic powder
Sea salt
Oil

For the labneh

You'll need to hang the labneh a day before serving this dish to ensure all the whey has been removed. Place all the ingredients in a mixing bowl and combine thoroughly, adding salt to taste. Transfer the mixture to a large piece of muslin cloth and wrap tightly, tying the top with string. Suspend the mix in the fridge with a bowl underneath to catch the whey and leave for 24 hours. Discard the whey and scrape the labneh from the muslin cloth into a clean container before use.

For the pickled onion

Pour the pickling liquor over the sliced onion and store in an airtight container. This is best done the day before, or left for even longer if you enjoy a sharp pickle.

For the koftas

Thoroughly combine the lamb with the spices, mint sauce and garlic powder in a mixing bowl. Shape into 18 equal sausage shapes, drizzle with a little oil, and season with salt. Cook the koftas under a preheated grill or on a hot barbecue for 10 minutes, turning them 45 degrees every 2 and a half minutes to brown evenly. Set them aside to rest for 5 minutes, then plate up alongside the labneh and pickled onion.

DUCK BREAST, CONFIT LEG SPRING ROLL, PICKLED BLACKBERRIES, ANISE CARROTS, CRISPY KALE

SERVES 6

This is a more complicated dish with a few elements going on, but good preparation will make for a showstopping Asian-inspired feast. Plump, late-harvest blackberries pickle so beautifully they almost take on a spiciness which lends itself so well to duck. A dry pan is the secret to great duck breast; the fat renders from the skin as it cooks, basting the meat. My method results in a pink duck breast, which when well rested is absolutely the best way to enjoy it, but adjust the timings if that's not for you. Brik pastry is a thin filo-like pastry from Tunisia, readily available and easy to work with.

200g blackberries
300ml pickling liquor (see page 249)
200ml vegetable oil (approx.)
150g green kale, leaves only
6 duck breasts

For the spring rolls
2 duck legs
50g sea salt
4 cloves of garlic, crushed
6 black peppercorns
4 juniper berries & 4 sprigs of thyme
½ an orange, peeled
500g duck fat
Rapeseed oil
3 sheets of brik pastry

For the sauce
Offal from 1 duck (neck, wings and giblets)
1 stick of celery, carrot & onion, chopped
1 bay leaf
125ml Port
500ml chicken stock
1 tsp Chinese five spice

For the carrots
3 carrots, trimmed, peeled and halved
2 tbsp honey
4 star anise

1 week in advance, place the blackberries in a sterilised airtight container or jar and pour over the pickling liquor. The crispy kale can be done in advance too. Heat the vegetable oil in a large saucepan until a piece of kale sizzles. Working in batches, deep fry the kale for about 1 minute before removing and draining on kitchen roll. Season liberally with salt.

For the spring rolls

Place the duck legs into a large container and rub with the salt, garlic, peppercorns, juniper, thyme, and orange peel. Cover and cure in the fridge overnight. First thing in the morning, rinse the cure off the duck legs and pat dry. Preheat your oven to 160°c and melt the duck fat in a deep roasting tin or cast-iron pot. Carefully add the duck legs to the fat, topping up with rapeseed oil if they aren't fully submerged. Cook in the oven for 2 hours or until the meat falls easily off the bone. Set the confit duck legs aside on kitchen roll and once cool enough to handle, pick the meat from the bones and shred with a fork. Reserve 3 tablespoons of the fat. Cut the brik pastry sheets in half and lightly brush the edges with water. Place the shredded duck meat along the sheet just off from the centre and fold the ends over, then roll tightly, wetting the edges a little more if they refuse to stick. Place in the fridge until needed.

For the sauce and carrots

Heat some rapeseed oil in a pan on a medium heat, then add the offal. Season with salt and cook for 10 minutes or until thoroughly browned. Add the chopped celery, carrot, onion, and bay leaf and cook for a further 10 minutes. Pour in the Port, bring to the boil and reduce by half, then add the stock and repeat. Turn the heat down and whisk in the five spice, simmering gently for 5 minutes. Meanwhile, roast the carrots with the honey, star anise, a pinch of salt and a drizzle of oil for 30 minutes at 180°c, turning halfway through.

For the duck breasts

Heat an ovenproof frying pan on a medium heat. Pat the skin dry with kitchen roll and season with salt. Lay skin side down in the hot dry pan and cook on a medium heat for 8 minutes, or until the fat is golden and crispy. Flip the breasts over and sear for a minute until browned, then turn back onto the skin side and place in the preheated oven for 7 minutes. Rest for 10 minutes before carving. Fry the spring rolls in the reserved confit fat until golden and crispy all over. Drain on kitchen roll before serving with all the other elements.

SQUIRREL RAGOUT PAPPARDELLE

SERVES 4

Invasive grey squirrels are environmentally destructive, and more efforts must be made to control their population, which in turn leaves us with a great deal of wild meat that often goes to waste. You can buy wild squirrel meat quite easily these days, and I strongly encourage that we increase demand for it. It is a delicious, lightly gamey meat that's also undeniably sustainable, good value and surprisingly easy to cook, especially as a braise for a hearty ragout sauce.

For the pangrattato

75g unsalted butter
200g panko breadcrumbs
1 tbsp chopped curly parsley
1½ tsp garlic powder

For the squirrel braise

4 grey squirrels, cleaned and any offal removed
1 stick of celery, carrot & onion, roughly chopped
1 bulb of garlic, split in half
6 black peppercorns
2 sprigs of thyme & 1 bay leaf
1 litre chicken stock

For the ragout sauce

1 stick of celery, carrot & onion, finely diced
3 cloves of garlic, grated
1 tbsp lilliput capers & 1 tsp fennel seeds
1 tbsp vinegar from a tin of pickled walnuts
125ml red wine
400g tinned plum tomatoes
Rapeseed oil
Sea salt

To serve

350g fresh pappardelle
100g semi-hard sheep's cheese such as Sheep Rustler (or pecorino)

For the pangrattato

You can make this in advance. First, melt the butter in a large frying pan. Once foaming, add the breadcrumbs and cook until golden brown, stirring often, then drain on a piece of kitchen roll. Once cool, transfer the crumbs to a mixing bowl and sprinkle evenly with the chopped parsley and garlic powder, seasoning with a little fine salt. Store in an airtight container until needed.

For the squirrel braise

Preheat your oven to 160°c. Place the squirrels in a deep roasting tin and add the chopped vegetables, halved garlic bulb, peppercorns, thyme, and bay leaf.

Pour the stock over the contents of the tin and if necessary, top up with enough water to ensure everything is fully covered. Cover the tin with foil and place in the oven for 3-4 hours, or until the meat is easily falling away from the bones.

Strain the braising liquor and set aside for later. Once cool enough to handle, pick the squirrel meat from the bones and set aside.

For the ragout sauce

Place a saucepan over a medium heat and add a dash of rapeseed oil. Add the celery, carrot, and onion to the pan, season with salt and cook until lightly caramelised.

Stir in the garlic, capers and fennel seeds and cook for a further 2-3 minutes. Deglaze the pan with the walnut vinegar, scraping any stuck-on bits off the bottom, then add the wine and bring to the boil. Let the liquid reduce by two thirds, then add the plum tomatoes and use a spoon to break them down. Add 250ml of the reserved squirrel braising liquor and simmer for an hour or until the sauce thickens to a ragout-like consistency. Add the squirrel meat 5 minutes before serving.

To serve

Place a pan of salted water on a high heat and bring to a rapid rolling boil. Add the fresh pappardelle and cook for 3 minutes, then drain. Add the pappardelle to the ragout and turn it through the sauce. Split between 4 bowls and finish with the sheep's cheese grated over the top.

BUFFALO RICOTTA GNUDI, SQUASH, SAGE BUTTER, WALNUT PESTO

SERVES 6

Gnudi – ricotta-based dumplings heralding from Tuscany – make a great lighter alternative to the better known potato-based gnocchi. I was introduced to gnudi by Mike who worked in the kitchen with me across the Autumn and winter of 2021-22, and I have to say it might be one of my all-time favourite vegetarian dishes that we've done. Despite his love for cooking, Mike left to follow his true passion for growing vegetables and now works at one of the Northwest's finest organic market gardens supplying top restaurants. He is also one of the loveliest people I've met, so thanks Mike; this one's for you.

For the gnudi

500g buffalo ricotta cheese
100g Spenwood or parmesan, grated
240g plain flour, plus extra for dusting
2 egg yolks
Sea salt

For the pesto

30g flat leaf parsley leaves
30g oregano leaves
30g sage leaves
50g walnuts
50g Spenwood or parmesan, grated
2 cloves of garlic, peeled
150ml extra virgin olive oil

For the sage butter and squash

1 clove of garlic, grated
10 fresh sage leaves, finely shredded
100g unsalted butter, softened
1 large onion squash
Rapeseed oil

For the gnudi

Firstly, wrap the ricotta in muslin cloth and squeeze to remove any excess water. In a mixing bowl, combine the ricotta, grated cheese, flour, and egg yolks. Season with salt and mix until a smooth, sticky dough forms. Dust a clean work surface with some plain flour. Take small portions of the dough and roll them into long, thin sausages. Cut the sausages into 2cm pieces and roll them into spheres, then set them aside on a floured tray.

Bring a large saucepan of salted water to a boil. Carefully drop the gnudi into the boiling water and cook for 2-3 minutes, or until they float to the surface, then remove with a slotted spoon and set aside to be finished later.

For the pesto

Put the herbs, walnuts, cheese, and garlic in a food processor. Pulse until combined. With the food processor running, slowly pour in the olive oil until the mixture is smooth. Season to taste and set aside to dress the plates.

For the sage butter and squash

Preheat your oven to 180°c. Fold the grated garlic and sage leaves into the softened butter and season with a little salt to taste.

Leaving the skin on, deseed the squash and cut into wedges. Place them on a baking tray, drizzle with rapeseed oil and season with salt, then roast for 20 minutes in the preheated oven until soft.

Place a deep sided frying pan on a medium heat and just as the squash comes out of the oven, add a good knob of sage butter to the pan along with the gnudi. Turn them every 30 seconds or so to ensure they colour evenly, then add the roast squash and toss through, allowing it to blacken a little before adding more sage butter. Remove from the heat and serve, dressed with the walnut pesto and a little more grated hard cheese if you wish.

MUSSELS COOKED IN BEER WITH BACON & CELERIAC

SERVES 6

Mussels always strike me as a summery ingredient, but they are truly at their best in Autumn and winter once their summer spawning is over. During the summer the flesh can be a little flabby and lacking in flavour as the mussel moves its energy elsewhere. This dish originates from very early on in the life of the pub when we would run fish specials on a Friday night. It was an opportunity for me to stretch my creative legs as well as test the water among our guests and regulars with new ideas. Fish Friday was always a great evening, and this dish is easily replicated at home for those who miss it.

2.5kg mussels, debearded and cleaned

100g unsalted butter

125g smoked streaky bacon, cut into small lardons

125g celeriac, peeled and finely diced

6 banana shallots, finely diced

4 cloves of garlic, grated

2 bay leaves

200ml brown ale

5 tbsp crème fraiche

1 tbsp finely chopped chervil

1 tbsp finely chopped curly parsley

Sea salt

Rinse the mussels in a colander under cold running water, discarding any with broken shells and those that don't close when tapped.

Melt the butter in a large saucepan over a medium heat and fry the bacon lardons until the fat begins to render. Add the celeriac, shallots, garlic, and bay leaves to the bacon, then fry for a further 6 minutes until soft. Now add the mussels and brown ale, cover with a lid, and cook for 5 minutes, shaking the pan occasionally.

Strain the mussels into a colander over a bowl or jug to reserve the cooking liquid. Discard any unopened mussels and pour the cooking liquor into a clean pan on a high heat. Bring to the boil and reduce by a third, then stir in the crème fraiche and chopped herbs.

Season the sauce with sea salt to taste, then add the drained mussels and reheat for a few seconds before serving. Enjoy alongside a loaf of crusty bread.

FISH STEW

SERVES 4

Everyone has their own version of a fish stew. They're all slightly similar, so my version probably stands out for the inclusion of brown crab meat. This is the meat found in the top of the shell of a crab and is quite the antithesis of delicate, sweet white crab meat from the legs and claws. The brown meat is intense and almost muddy in flavour with a deep earthy shellfish smell. It is a perfect match for this sweet, tomato-heavy stew. Ensuring the squid tentacles have the time to braise is also key, otherwise they will remain chewy and rubbery.

Rapeseed oil
1 large fennel bulb, finely chopped
3 banana shallots, finely chopped
2 sticks of celery, finely chopped
4 cloves of garlic, thinly sliced
1 small red chilli, deseeded and thinly sliced
2 star anise
2 tsp fennel seeds
2 tsp smoked paprika
¼ tsp cayenne pepper
A pinch of saffron
175ml white wine
650g ripe red and orange tomatoes, peeled, deseeded and chopped
500ml fish stock
100g brown crab meat
Tentacles from 2 squid, cleaned
750g cod fillet, skinned, boned and cut into 4cm pieces
300g mussels, debearded and cleaned
½ lemon
Sea salt
1 bunch of chervil leaves, chopped

Heat a splash of rapeseed oil in a large cast iron casserole dish over a medium-low heat. Add the chopped fennel, shallots and celery and cook gently, stirring often, for 15 minutes until soft.

Add the sliced garlic and chilli, star anise, fennel seeds, paprika, cayenne pepper, and saffron to the casserole dish and stir in thoroughly. Cook on a low heat for a further 5 minutes.

Now add the white wine and turn the heat up, bringing it to a boil. Reduce the volume of liquid by a quarter, then add the tomatoes and reduce the heat to cook very gently, stirring occasionally, for about 30 minutes. After this time, pour in the fish stock and simmer for a further 10 minutes.

Add the brown crab meat and squid tentacles to the stew, stir through and cook for 40 minutes.

Meanwhile, season the prepared cod with salt and allow it to cure for 10 minutes.

After the 40 minutes, add the mussels to the stew and cover with a lid. Let it cook for 3 minutes before you uncover, stir, and add the lightly cured cod. Cover again and cook on a low heat for a further 4-5 minutes until the fish is just cooked and the mussels are open. Discard any unopened mussels. Squeeze over the juice from the halved lemon and stir in the chervil leaves, seasoning to taste as required. Enjoy with good bread.

ROAST SIRLOIN OF BEEF

SERVES 4-6

I love beef sirloin. Flavourful, great texture, more forgiving than lean fillet and easier to cook than fat-rich rib roasts, it's been our beef joint of choice at The Pack Horse since day one. A good butcher will remove the sinew under the fat for you and roll it securely with the fat cap intact, which is crucial for keeping the joint moist, and provides a lovely salty treat. Fat always means flavour and should be enjoyed in moderation. From an outdoor reared cow raised on natural pasture, dry-aged for at least 28 days, you'll find nothing better.

1.5kg boned and rolled sirloin joint
1 large onion, peeled
2 carrots, peeled
2 sticks of celery
2 sprigs of thyme
1 bay leaf
Sea salt
Rapeseed or vegetable oil

Remove the sirloin from the fridge and allow it to come up to room temperature. Preheat your oven to 210°c.

Roughly chop the onion, carrot and celery into big chunks and place in a roasting tin, then scatter over the thyme and bay. Place the sirloin on top, positioned centrally in the tin, then liberally cover with sea salt and drizzle the entire contents of the roasting tin with oil.

Place in the oven for 15 minutes, then remove and turn the oven down to 160°c. When the oven is cool enough, place the tray back in for 35 minutes. If you're using a meat thermometer, 50°c in the centre is a perfect medium-rare.

Remove the sirloin from the oven, loosely cover with tin foil and leave to rest for 20 minutes. During that time, place the tray of vegetables back into the oven and continue to roast for a delicious additional side dish. Carve the beef into slices following the shape and direction of the joint to serve.

CURRIED GOAT PIE

SERVES 6

This was one of our Covid-19 comeback dishes, as well as part of our Pack Horse At Home boxes which we provided during lockdown. I have James Whetlor to thank for this, for introducing me to a sustainable meat that we should all be eating more of, and for pointing me in the right direction when it comes to cooking it well! James left River Cottage to set up Cabrito Goat Meat, an ethical meat company which puts billy goats born into the dairy industry back into the food chain. His work has transformed the industry and our consumption of goat meat, and it's a pleasure to play a small part in that.

500g pie pastry (I recommend hot water pastry – see page 250)

2 egg yolks, beaten

For the marinated goat

1.2kg diced kid goat

250ml plain yoghurt

3 cardamom pods

2 cloves

2 star anise

1 cinnamon stick

1 tbsp cumin seeds

1 tbsp coriander seeds

1 tbsp paprika

2 tsp sea salt

1 tsp curry powder

1 tsp cayenne pepper

For the curry sauce

2 red onions, roughly chopped

2 tsp garlic paste

1 tsp ginger paste

Stalks from 15g fresh coriander

50g unsalted butter

1 tsp curry powder

½ tsp garam masala

2 tbsp tomato paste

400g tinned plum tomatoes

Rapeseed oil

For the marinated goat

Lightly toast the cardamom, cloves, star anise, cinnamon, cumin, and coriander in a frying pan until aromatic, then leave to cool.

Mix the diced goat with the yoghurt, toasted whole spices, paprika, salt, curry powder, and cayenne pepper. Leave to marinate for at least 2 hours, but preferably overnight.

For the curry sauce

Heat some oil in a pan and then add the onion, garlic paste, ginger paste, and coriander stalks. Cook slowly until soft, then add the butter, curry powder and garam masala. Cook for a further 10 minutes before blitzing to a rough paste and turning the heat right down.

Preheat your oven to 240°c. Spread the marinated goat meat out in a couple of roasting tins and place in the oven for 15 minutes. Transfer the hot goat meat along with all the marinade to the pan of curry sauce, turning it through the blitzed paste and butter. Add the tomato paste and tinned tomatoes, then rinse the tin with a splash of water and add it to the pan. Cook on a very low heat for 3 hours, stirring occasionally to ensure even cooking and stop anything burning on the base.

Lightly grease a 20cm pie tin with butter and roll out your pastry to 3mm thickness. Lay the pastry into the tin, pressing it gently into the sides all the way around. Chill in the fridge for 30 minutes.

Preheat your oven to 190°c. Fill your lined pie tin with the curried goat and top with a pie lid rolled out from the remaining pastry. Crimp the edges, then brush the beaten egg yolk over the lid with a pastry brush. Place the pie in the preheated oven to cook for 30 minutes, then it's ready to serve.

LAMB SHOULDER WITH MERGUEZ SPICES, BRAISED FENNEL, CUCUMBER & WALNUT TARATOR

SERVES 6-8

I love lamb shoulders. They are a great example of how effortless and rewarding slow cooking can be, and lamb really lends itself to the robust African merguez spice blend used here. Tarator – a chilled Bulgarian soup – works deliciously as a dressing, similar to tzatziki but with an earthy undertone to really blend in with the spices on display.

For the tarator

Sea salt

2 cucumbers, deseeded and diced

500ml natural yoghurt

4 cloves of garlic, grated

3 tbsp crushed walnuts

1 bunch of dill, shredded

For the lamb

2 cloves

1 tsp fennel seeds

1 tsp cumin seeds

1 tsp coriander seeds

1 tsp black peppercorns

½ cinnamon stick, broken up

A pinch of cayenne pepper

1 tsp garlic powder

2 tsp smoked paprika

2 tsp sea salt

2 tsp rapeseed oil

1 bone-in shoulder of lamb

For the braised fennel

2 large fennel bulbs, sliced into 4 wedges each

2 cloves of garlic, peeled and crushed

1 tsp coriander seeds

1 tsp fennel seeds

1 bay leaf

For the tarator

Make this the day before to allow the flavours to come together. On a baking sheet, lightly salt the diced cucumber and leave to sit for 20 minutes. Pour away any excess water, rinse, pat dry, then place in a mixing bowl. Add the yoghurt, garlic, walnuts, and dill. Mix thoroughly and then place in the fridge overnight.

For the lamb

In a dry frying pan over a medium heat, toast the cloves, fennel, cumin, coriander, peppercorns, and cinnamon for a minute. Crush to a coarse powder using a pestle and mortar, then combine with the cayenne, garlic powder, paprika, salt and oil. Set aside.

Preheat your oven to 230°c. Lightly score the skin of the lamb shoulder with a sharp knife, ensuring you keep the slashes shallow, barely piercing the flesh. Rub half the spice paste all over the lamb shoulder, pressing it into the cuts. Place the shoulder into a roasting tin and cook in the oven for 30 minutes. Remove from the oven and reduce the heat to 120°c. Using a wooden spoon, rub the remaining spice paste all over the shoulder. Add a glass of water to the tin, loosely cover with foil and return to the oven for 6 hours. Remove from the oven and pull the shoulder blade from the meat. This should yield easily and is a good indicator that the meat is well cooked. Leave to rest for 30 minutes under the foil.

For the braised fennel

While the lamb rests, place the fennel wedges in a pan with the garlic, seeds, and bay leaf. Add enough water to just cover the fennel. Cook on a high heat until soft and tender, then remove and lay on a baking tray. If you have a blowtorch, gently flame the fennel just enough to char the outside. If not, place under a hot grill for 5 minutes.

To serve

Drizzle the braised fennel with the tarator. Pull the meat from the lamb shoulder with some forks and lay on a warmed plate, drizzling over the juices from the pan.

LEMON CAKE

MAKES 1 LOAF CAKE

This was the first cake I ever baked on my own, and the original recipe is still out there somewhere on a blog I used to write which was half university project, half documenting my early forays into cookery. Now, we enjoy this on crisp autumnal days with a strong cup of tea, gazing out of the window as Hayfield transforms before us. The apricot glaze makes all the difference here; perhaps if you've made your own apricot jam over the summer, you can elevate it even further than I can.

For the cake

100g unsalted butter
5 free-range eggs
300g caster sugar
140ml double cream
30ml spiced rum
3 lemons, zested
A pinch of salt
240g plain flour
½ tsp baking powder

For the apricot glaze

3 tbsp apricot jam
1 lemon, zested and juiced
150g icing sugar

For the cake

Preheat your oven to 180°c and lightly butter a 26cm x 9cm x 8cm (standard size) loaf tin. In a small saucepan, melt the butter and leave to cool slightly without letting it reset.

In a large mixing bowl, whisk the melted butter with the eggs, sugar, cream, rum, lemon zest, and salt, then sift in the flour and baking powder. Continue to whisk for 2-3 minutes until the mixture is smooth. The more you whisk, the more air you will fold into the mix, creating a lighter sponge once cooked.

Pour the mixture into the prepared tin and bake in the preheated oven for 50-60 minutes, turning the tin around halfway through cooking. The best way to see if it's cooked is to insert a knife into the centre of the cake; if it comes out clean, it's ready. Remove the cake from the tin, turn onto a cooling rack and leave to cool for 10 minutes. Leave the oven turned on as you will need it again shortly.

For the apricot glaze

Warm the apricot jam in a saucepan and brush it evenly over the cooled cake. To complete the glaze, combine the lemon zest and juice with the icing sugar in the pan and heat gently until you have a smooth liquid. Brush this over the cake, covering it completely.

Place the glazed cake in the oven on a baking tray, turn off the heat and leave for 6 minutes to dry the glaze and turn it translucent. Remove from the oven and leave the cake to cool completely before serving in thick slices.

HEATHER PANNA COTTA, MACERATED PEACHES

SERVES 6

This is a lovely uplifting dessert which uses the beautiful blooming heather that surrounds Hayfield in the summer to give the classic panna cotta a floral note. Fresh, juicy, summer peaches are a true seasonal delight, and when lightly macerated they just come alive with sweet-sharp stone fruit flavour.

For the heather panna cotta

600ml double cream

225ml whole milk

90g caster sugar

50g heather tops, washed

1 vanilla pod, split lengthways

3½ sheets of bronze leaf gelatine

For the macerated peaches

4 peaches, stoned and sliced

3 sprigs of thyme, leaves only

1 tbsp caster sugar

1 lemon, juiced

For the heather panna cotta

Pour the cream, milk and sugar into a saucepan, then add the heather tops and vanilla seeds, scraping them into the mixture from the split pod with a knife. Stir to combine and gently bring to a steaming simmer, then remove from the heat and take out the heather tops with a slotted spoon.

Soak the gelatine in a bowl of cold water for 5 minutes, then squeeze out the excess liquid and stir the softened gelatine into the warm panna cotta mix until fully dissolved. Pour the mix into your serving dishes and leave to set in the fridge for 3 hours.

For the macerated peaches

Place the sliced peaches in a bowl and sprinkle the thyme leaves and sugar over them. Squeeze over the lemon juice, stirring to combine. Cover the bowl with cling film and let the peaches sit for an hour in the fridge. Just before serving, turn the peaches through the juice in the bowl once more.

To serve, spoon the macerated peaches on top of the set panna cotta along with a little of their juice.

GREENGAGE CLAFOUTIS

SERVES 4

Lovely tart greengages are among the first of the plum cultivars to provide fruit for us in late summer. Prepared here in a simple but classic clafoutis – which is traditionally made with cherries – this recipe is a great way to use up a glut of fruit from the garden. The plum liqueur is optional but does give the fruit a rich and boozy kick.

For the macerated greengages
500g greengages, stoned and halved
100g caster sugar
50ml plum liqueur

For the clafoutis
20g unsalted butter, plus extra for greasing
50g caster sugar, plus extra for dusting
2 eggs
½ tsp vanilla paste
20g plain flour
50ml whole milk
75ml double cream
Sea salt

For the macerated greengages

Place the halved greengages in a mixing bowl, add the sugar and plum liqueur, then stir to coat them thoroughly. Cover with cling film and allow to macerate in the fridge for 2 hours.

For the clafoutis

Preheat your oven to 180°c. Grease a 20cm ovenproof dish with unsalted butter, then dust with a little caster sugar. In a large bowl, whisk the sugar, eggs and vanilla together until creamy. Melt the butter in a small saucepan and heat until foaming, then take it straight off the heat and set aside.

Add the flour to the egg and sugar mixture and whisk until smooth, then slowly pour in the milk, cream, and foaming butter with a pinch of sea salt.

Stir the greengages and their macerating juices into the clafoutis batter, then pour the mix into your prepared baking dish. Place in the preheated oven and bake for 30 minutes.

Serve the greengage clafoutis hot from the oven and enjoy with a dollop of clotted cream.

CHOCOLATE & BEETROOT BROWNIES

SERVES 6

This recipe is for Neve, who we inherited when we took over the pub. She was 15 years old at the time and did a little waitressing alongside manning the wall of panini grills in the kitchen. Once we took over, Neve agreed to stay and work front of house, and there she stayed until October 2022, working her way up to shift leader while achieving first class honours at university along the way. I put these brownies on the menu for a brief stint in early 2017, and it was the first and possibly only time I had seen Neve eat a vegetable and truly enjoy it. It was our great pleasure to see Neve grow up, and she will forever be part of The Pack Horse family.

350g beetroot

250g unsalted butter, cubed

250g dark chocolate (about 70% cocoa solids)

3 eggs

250g caster sugar

150g wholemeal self-raising flour

A pinch of sea salt

In a medium saucepan, bring lightly salted water to the boil, then add the beetroot and cook until soft. Remove from the water, peel and grate, then set aside.

Line a baking tin with baking parchment and preheat your oven to 180°c. Bring a pan of water to the boil, then reduce to a simmer. Place a mixing bowl over the top and gently melt the butter and chocolate together, stirring continuously.

In a separate mixing bowl, whisk the eggs and sugar together, then pour the melted chocolate and butter over the top, whisking continuously until combined. Gently fold in the flour and then the salt, followed by the grated beetroot. Don't overmix otherwise your brownies will be hard.

Pour the mixture into the lined tin and bake in the preheated oven for 22 minutes. Using the parchment, lift the brownies out onto a cooling rack. Once cooled, cut into squares and enjoy.

FRONT OF HOUSE
AT THE PACK HORSE

There is a certain challenge that comes with finding the balance between being a friendly local pub and serving the kind of food that we serve, and that is where our front of house team truly shine. When it was just me and Emma working together after opening The Pack Horse, Emma made a point of getting to know as many locals as possible, and she has a gift for remembering names and faces along with the respective dogs in tow. She always wanted it to be a local place for local people, which I will admit I lost sight of on a few occasions as the food offer developed. The key to our success came with Emma bringing in her knowledge of relaxed but attentive, friendly, and familiar service. Under Emma's stewardship, the same core beliefs of those early days at the pub still ring true in our current front of house team.

It's important for us to avoid an atmosphere of stuffiness or pretentiousness; a good pub is open and welcoming to everyone regardless of the food it serves. The front section of The Pack Horse, surrounding a traditional wood burning stove, is never set up as part of the restaurant and cannot be booked. This gives us a guaranteed area for around 20 people who may just wish to come in for a quiet drink, and we'd never want to take that away from them. We also actively encourage punters to sit at the bar, and it is always lovely to see familiar faces there on a regular basis. Our open kitchen looks out onto the entire pub, and our locals interact with the chefs from a distance, eventually getting to know them personally.

We love the community spirit this interaction drives, giving everything a higher purpose. I've said from the start that this pub has been part of the local community for a lot longer than we've been here, so it is of utmost importance that we respect that. It begins with a simple smile and greeting on arrival: first impressions count for so much. We guide people through the drinks available, offering free tasters and helping to inform their decision. A little detail and a small price to pay for ensuring everyone who comes to our bar has a lovely time and gets served a drink that we know they'll really enjoy. We also run a weekly quiz night every Wednesday and serve bar snacks; we love this as it's almost like a night just for the locals: stripped back, simple and great fun, which is just what a proper pub should feel like.

Matt, Emma's brother, has also become instrumental in driving forward our front of house standards. Matt joined the team in 2021, having spent most of his life living on the Isle of Bute in Scotland; his parents had moved there and taken a very young Matthew with them while Emma was at university in Sheffield. They briefly lived together at Emma's house in Sheffield, but the combination of young professional and teenage angst made their relationship volatile and when Matt asked to join the team at The Pack Horse temporarily while he came up with a long-term plan, there was initially a little reluctance. Matt was between jobs, houses, and relationships though, and we could offer him a spare room to live in and provide a little stability after a challenging time throughout the pandemic. It was the right thing to do as family.

As it turned out, Matt had a natural ability on the floor and with the guests that was evident almost immediately. Thanks to his efforts in learning our locals' names, much like his sister had done before, the village warmed to him very quickly. In fact, he now knows the locals so well he will often be pouring their drinks before they've even had chance to order them. His charm with diners made him very likeable, but as the weeks ticked by, something else sparked within him. A sudden love of wine had bloomed, seemingly out of nowhere. Matt himself professed to have never enjoyed wine – it would have been one of the last things he'd drink – but as we transitioned our wine list to match our food offering, everything changed for him. His passion grew so much that he undertook his WSET wine exams and passed with distinction. Not only was he good with locals and diners, Matt also gained an immense amount of knowledge and confidence to back that up. A self-taught love of food and beer in combination with his passion for wine, a natural ability to read people, and an understanding of the workings of our pub and restaurant as one entity have made him practically unstoppable. What started off as a three month offer of a little help has now entered its third year.

Behind Matt are his equally professional and driven front of house colleagues who excel in their own ways, creating a dream team when all their respective strengths are played to. Jodie rules in the office with her organisational work, Gabby bounces around the restaurant effortlessly and has become our quiz master, Amy brightens everyone's day and can even calm a stormy kitchen simply with her presence. Our full-time team are supported by a group of local young people, a great advantage of small village life. Not only are they all great, but they already know everybody having been born and raised here, and it is almost a village event for their families and friends to come visit the pub while they're working behind the bar. It is a true celebration of rural life within a small village, and it is a pleasure to be part of that enrichment within the local community.

Winter

The nights draw in, the trees stand empty and alone, there is a deafening silence carried on an icy wind, and all is still. Winter is upon us. Nature has retreated from such hostility; even the birds have forsaken the world around us. But under the surface, nature's resilience still provides.

The bounty of Autumn swiftly becomes a distant memory in the bleak midwinter. Kales, cabbages and sprouts dominate the vegetable patch, their tightly wound parcels of leaves a perfect defence against sudden temperature drops. Under the soil, celeriac and turnips are now full of an entire year of change, a robust and intense reflection of the world around them: resilient, tough, full of flavour.

This theme continues among all winter vegetables, though there is a glimmer of hope. Hard at work in cavernous sheds across Yorkshire, generations of farmers tend to their crop by candlelight. And suddenly, like a light in the darkness, the first pink spears of forced rhubarb arrive. Finally, a riposte to the hardy savouriness of Winter.

Creativity is key in the winter kitchen. We have a responsibility to keep our guests happy, so our menu is at its most deep and rich, utilising the strong flavours available to us. However, it is also a time of preservation, where late-harvest summer and Autumn fruits are pickled for us to use throughout the Winter. Without them, the wait for bright rhubarb would be a far less bearable struggle.

Here feel we not the penalty of Adam,
The seasons' difference, as the icy fang
And churlish chiding of the winter's wind,
Which, when it bites and blows upon my body,
Even till I shrink with cold, I smile.

From As You Like It, William Shakespeare

OUR SEASONAL HIGHLIGHTS

DECEMBER
Celeriac

Salsify

Sprouts

Potatoes

JANUARY
Pears

Turnips

Forced rhubarb

January King cabbage

FEBRUARY
Chicory

Monk's beard

Field mushrooms

Jerusalem artichoke

Lantern Pike

3½ MILES, MODERATE, 373M SUMMIT, ALLOW 2–2½ HOURS.

A local hilltop with 360° views. One stiff climb halfway through. Surfaces may be muddy after rain, and slightly rocky in places. There are several stiles along this route, including a narrow section of wall. One field is periodically used for grazing cattle. If confronted, release any dogs and head for the nearest exit in the opposite direction of the cows.

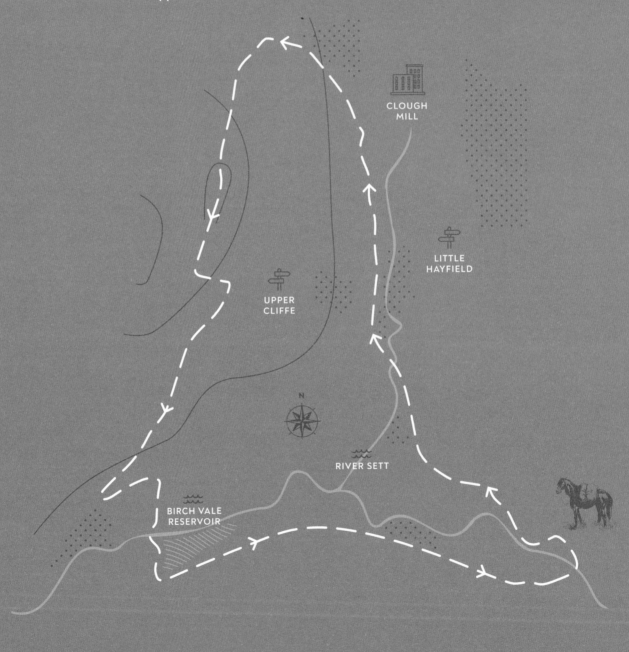

This route begins along the Sett Valley Trail, which forms part of the Pennine Bridleway. This was formerly the Hayfield – New Mills Branch line; the old Hayfield station site is now the Sett Valley car park and trail information centre. Lantern Pike is a great introductory peak, providing extensive views of Greater Manchester and the Sett Valley along with a unique perspective of Hayfield's place in the rolling landscape.

From the front of The Pack Horse, turn left along Market Street to the war memorial and then bear right over the bridge across the River Sett. Turn right (signposted to the Sett Valley Trail) and walk past the church to the village bypass. Cross with care at the lights. Walk through the car park and, at the far end, join the Sett Valley Trail, following the former branch line from New Mills to Hayfield. Follow the Trail through a gate and past a house on the right by a former level crossing. Pass above a small reservoir to your right and then, when a path crosses, turn right off the Trail signposted "Lantern Pike 1 mile".

Follow the footpath around the bottom of the reservoir and cross the River Sett. Climb the grassy bank beyond and head for a gate in the corner of the field left of a farmhouse. After a narrow, fenced-off section, you reach a wall stile into the farm drive. Turn left. Walk past some chicken houses on your right, then follow the drive round a sharp right-hand bend, ignoring

the descending bridleway straight ahead. Continue along the gently ascending track until you reach Sitch Lane. Turn right, then immediately left up a no-through road with a Pennine Bridleway sign. Climb steeply to a house, ignoring the turning to Higher Cliffe Farm on your right, and then continue along the bridleway beyond. Just after a gate, turn left off the main track by a National Trust sign, and climb a narrow path beside a wall. At the top of the slope, turn right along the ridge towards the top of Lantern Pike.

Beyond the topograph at the summit, follow the path ahead that descends through heather to rejoin the Pennine Bridleway. Follow a short section of walled track left to a gate into open fields. Head out into the field, then bear right over the brow of the hill to a stile in the bottom corner. The path beyond leads steeply downhill beside a wood, then continues between bilberry-clad walls. A stile at the end leads into a driveway between two houses.

Turn right along the track, ignoring a footpath leading down the grassy slope towards Little Hayfield. Pass another farmhouse and ignore a path off to the right. At a hairpin bend, continue along the bridleway ahead. At a gate, leave the bridleway to follow a footpath on the left that descends above trees to cross the stream between stone cottages. Follow the metalled lane beyond. At the junction, turn left past the entrances to Swallow House Crescent on your left, then The Glade and Wood Gardens on your right (opposite Lea Road). Turn right into the May Queen Field (recreation ground) before you reach the bypass overbridge and stay left, following the river upstream under the bypass. Continue between houses to emerge just to the right of The Pack Horse.

MUSHROOM RAGOUT, STRAW POTATOES, PICKLED WALNUT DRESSING, POACHED EGGS

SERVES 4

I'm sure you've noticed by now just how much I love pickled walnuts. This dressing adds even more of a vinegary kick to them: the perfect foil to the deeply earthy mushrooms and rich runny egg yolks. I'd enjoy this as a starter or a fancy breakfast but would certainly poach double the number of eggs for breakfast time. Perfect poached eggs require the largest saucepan in the house. It looks ridiculous but giving your eggs all that space makes the difference.

For the pickled walnut dressing

100ml good quality extra virgin olive oil
100g pickled walnuts
4 tbsp vinegar from the tin of pickled walnuts
50ml red wine vinegar
4 cloves of garlic
A pinch of sea salt

For the straw potatoes

300ml vegetable oil
2 potatoes, peeled

For the ragout

Rapeseed oil
50g unsalted butter
800g button mushrooms, sliced
3 cloves of garlic, grated
2 sprigs of thyme, leaves only
175ml Madeira
400ml chicken or vegetable stock
1 tbsp chopped curly parsley
1 tbsp chopped chervil
1 tbsp chopped chives

To serve

75ml white wine vinegar
4 eggs

For the pickled walnut dressing

You can make this in advance. Simply place all the ingredients into a food processor and blitz until smooth and emulsified. Store in an airtight container in the fridge until needed.

For the straw potatoes

You can also prepare these in advance. Heat the vegetable oil in a saucepan. Using a Japanese mandoline with the teeth attachment, carefully slice the potatoes into tiny straw ribbons. Wrap in a cheesecloth or thin tea towel and squeeze all the moisture out of them. Working in batches, carefully fry the potatoes in the hot oil until golden and then drain on a piece of kitchen roll. Season with salt and store in an airtight container until needed.

For the ragout

Heat some rapeseed oil in a saucepan. Once hot, melt the butter in the pan and then add the sliced mushrooms. Cook until softened, then add the garlic and thyme and cook for a further 10 minutes on a medium heat, drawing out the moisture from the mushrooms.

Add the Madeira to the pan and bring to the boil, then let the liquid reduce by three quarters. Pour in the stock and turn the heat down to medium, then allow it all to be absorbed and reduced to a sticky sauce which binds the mushrooms together. Stir all the chopped herbs through the ragout 1 minute before serving.

To serve

Fill your largest saucepan with water, add the vinegar and season with salt. Bring to the boil and then turn down to a gentle simmer where only a few bubbles are rising to the surface. Break the eggs in one at a time and leave undisturbed to poach for 3 minutes, then remove with a slotted spoon and carefully pat dry. Serve the poached eggs atop the mushroom ragout spotted with the pickled walnut dressing, then finish with the crispy straw potatoes.

POTATO & WINTER TRUFFLE SOUP

SERVES 6

This a hearty and wholesome bowl to warm you up in the long winter months. It's basically a very easy way to add another dimension to a classic leek and potato soup; truffle just brings that luxury earthiness to the finished dish.

Vegetable oil
100g celery, chopped
2 cloves of garlic, chopped
2 leeks, white parts only, sliced
800g potatoes, peeled and chopped
2 sprigs of thyme
2 bay leaves
1.5 litres vegetable stock
100ml white truffle oil
Sea salt

In a large pot, heat some oil over a medium heat. Add the celery, garlic, and leek to cook until soft and translucent. Stir in the chopped potatoes, thyme, and bay leaves before pouring in the vegetable stock. Stir well and bring to the boil, then reduce the heat and simmer for 20-25 minutes or until the potatoes are tender.

Remove the thyme sprigs and bay leaves from the pot, discarding them. Add half the truffle oil to the soup. Using an immersion blender, blend the soup until smooth. Alternatively, you can transfer the soup to a blender and blend in batches, then reheat in the pan if needed.

Season the soup with salt to taste and serve in bowls with an additional drizzle of truffle oil on top, plus some fresh truffle shavings if you have any.

CRISPY OX TONGUE, WINTER LEAF & LORD OF THE HUNDREDS CAESAR SALAD

SERVES 6

I love ox tongue. It's super lean, flavoursome and great value for money. It is something we should really eat more of outside the classic sandwich filling. It's also surprisingly easy to cook when bought whole and pre-brined from a good local butcher. Winter leaves have such a delicate mustardy bitterness to them which combine well with the intensely savoury notes of a Caesar dressing. Lord of the Hundreds is a hard ewe's cheese from Sussex. The savoury flavour with a hint of roasted hazelnuts makes it a perfect parmesan alternative in this recipe.

For the Caesar dressing

150g Lord of the Hundreds
60ml white wine vinegar
1 lime, juiced
2 tsp Dijon mustard
12 salted anchovy fillets
200ml grapeseed oil
60ml extra virgin olive oil

For the tongue

1 ox tongue (approximately 700g)
1 onion, peeled and quartered
1 carrot, quartered
2 sticks of celery, roughly chopped
3 cloves of garlic, crushed
2 bay leaves
1 tbsp red wine vinegar
Sea salt
2 eggs, beaten
120g plain flour
120g panko breadcrumbs
Oil for frying

For the salad

1 head of Castelfranco, leaves torn
1 head of radicchio, leaves torn
2 heads of chicory, leaves torn
12 salted anchovy fillets
100g Lord of the Hundreds

For the Caesar dressing

You can make this in advance. Place the Lord of the Hundreds, vinegar, lime juice, mustard, and anchovies in a food processor and blitz to a paste. Combine the oils and gradually pour into the food processor, blitzing continuously as you go. Season to taste and store in a suitable container.

For the tongue

Rinse the ox tongue under cold water and remove any excess fat or membranes, then place in a large pot with enough water to cover it. Add the onion, carrot, celery, garlic, bay leaves, vinegar, and a generous pinch of salt to the pot. Bring to a simmer and cook for 2-3 hours, until the tongue is tender. Remove it from the pot and leave to cool slightly, then peel off the tough outer layer of skin and slice the tongue into 1cm thick pieces.

Put the eggs, flour and breadcrumbs into 3 separate dishes. Dip each piece of ox tongue into the flour, then into the beaten egg and finally into the breadcrumbs, making sure you coat each piece evenly. Heat the oil in a frying pan over medium-high heat. When the oil is hot, carefully add the breaded ox tongue pieces to the pan in batches, being careful not to overcrowd the pan. Fry the ox tongue for 3-4 minutes on each side, or until golden brown and crispy, then remove with a slotted spoon and place on a plate lined with paper towels to drain any excess oil.

For the salad

Dress all the torn winter leaves with your Caesar dressing, then top with the anchovy fillets, and finish with Lord of the Hundreds grated over the top. Serve alongside the crispy ox tongue.

CHICKEN LIVER PARFAIT, FARMHOUSE CHUTNEY

SERVES 8

This recipe featured on our opening menu back in September 2016, and is so good that it remained there until summer 2022. This is a classic French style parfait, richer and smoother than a pâté, and perhaps the first dish which subconsciously dictated the direction and identity of my style. The chutney is a fantastic all-rounder, perfect with cheese at Christmas. So good, in fact, that we might start making jars of it.

For the chutney

300g apple, peeled, cored and chopped
2 banana shallots, peeled and chopped
2 cloves of garlic, grated
250g tomatoes, chopped
200g pitted dates
200g raisins
200g soft dark brown sugar
40g root ginger, peeled and grated
120ml cider vinegar

For the parfait

400g chicken livers
300ml whole milk
300ml cold water
5g sea salt
100ml Madeira
100ml Port
50ml brandy
1 shallot, diced
4 sprigs of thyme, leaves only
1 clove of garlic, peeled
400g unsalted butter
10g Himalayan pink salt
5 eggs

For the chutney

This can be made days in advance, allowing time to bring the flavours together. Place all the ingredients in a large saucepan and cook on a gentle heat for around 1 hour 30 minutes, stirring often to avoid anything sticking. Leave to cool, then store in an airtight container in the fridge.

For the parfait

Soak the livers in the whole milk, water and sea salt for an hour to remove the bitterness, then drain. Preheat your oven to 120°c and line an ovenproof terrine mould with greaseproof paper.

Put all the alcohols in a pan with the shallot, thyme and garlic. Bring to the boil, reduce the volume of liquid by a third and then set aside. Melt the butter in a pan, then keep it warm on a very low heat. Place the drained livers in a food processor and blitz, adding the Himalayan pink salt and the reduced alcohol mixture. Keep the blender going and add the eggs one at a time, giving it an extra minute to blend after the final egg, then add the warm butter and blend until fully combined. Pass the mixture through a fine sieve into the terrine mould and cover with tin foil.

Place the terrine in a roasting tin and fill the tin about halfway up with boiling water. Bake in the preheated oven for 40 minutes and then chill over ice. Refrigerate overnight once cool.

Remove the terrine from its mould the following day, then serve in slices with hot buttered sourdough toast and a generous dollop of chutney.

CURED TROUT, BUTTERMILK BEURRE BLANC

SERVES 6

This is our little nod to a classical French dish, and a proper butter sauce is a great recipe for any cook to have in their repertoire. Finished with buttermilk and studded with lemony trout roe (ask your fishmonger to get hold of a jar for you, it's surprisingly affordable), this is a butter sauce with more sharpness than usual: the perfect balance for salty, fatty, cured trout.

1 x 800g side of chalk stream trout, skinned and pin bones removed

100g sea salt

100g soft brown sugar

210ml white wine

120ml white wine vinegar

60ml double cream

115g unsalted butter, cubed

60ml buttermilk

3 sprigs of curly parsley, finely chopped

3 sprigs of chervil, finely chopped

3 sprigs of dill, finely chopped

1 gherkin, finely diced

1 shallot, finely diced

1 tsp lilliput capers

¼ tsp herring roe

¼ tsp trout roe

Cure the fish a day before serving. Lay the trout on a tray and sprinkle evenly with the salt and sugar, turning the fish over to ensure an even cure. Drizzle 150ml of the white wine evenly over the top and cling film the tray. Leave to cure initially for 4 hours, then turn the fish over and cure for a further 4 hours. Wash the cure off under cold running water and pat the fish until bone dry, then wrap tightly in cling film and leave in the fridge.

When you want to serve the dish, portion the cured fish into 6 equal pieces and place on a baking tray. Using a cook's blowtorch, flame the top of the fish until the flakes appear charred, then place under a grill at a low heat while you finish the beurre blanc. If you don't have a blowtorch, pan fry the portions of fish top side down on a high heat for a few minutes to get a similar effect.

In a medium saucepan, combine the remaining 60ml of white wine with the white wine vinegar. Bring to the boil over a medium-high heat and reduce until there is about 2 tablespoons of liquid left. Add the cream and cook for another 5 minutes. Reduce the heat to low and whisk in the butter one cube at a time until the mixture is smooth and beginning to thicken. Stir in the buttermilk and season with salt to taste, then finish the sauce with the chopped herbs, diced gherkin and shallot, capers, and fish roes. Spoon onto a plate and place the trout on top.

ONION SQUASH STUFFED WITH SPELT, MUSHROOMS & BLUE CHEESE

SERVES 4

The loveliest thing about onion squash is that there's no faff in peeling them, as the skins are edible. They roast whole beautifully and look stunning with their blistered charred skins and spooky appearance. Spelt is very similar to pearl barley only a little nuttier in flavour and texture, a perfect match for the earthy mushrooms and blue cheese. This is a great Halloween family feast, and certainly helps get everyone in the mood for some pumpkin – or onion squash – carving.

4 medium-size onion squash

Sea salt

Rapeseed oil

250g spelt grain

1 bay leaf

50g unsalted butter

2 leeks, white parts thinly sliced

300g button mushrooms, trimmed and sliced

2 cloves of garlic, grated

1 bunch of curly parsley leaves, finely chopped

150g semi-soft blue cheese (such as Blue Murder)

Soured cream, to serve (optional)

Preheat your oven to 180°c. Using a sharp, heavy knife, carefully cut off the tops and bases of each squash, ensuring they can sit upright. Set the tops aside and discard the bases. With a metal spoon, gently scoop out the seeds and fibrous matter, leaving a neat hollow in each squash. Place on a baking tray with the tops and season the cavities with salt, then give them all a good drizzle of oil and place into the oven to roast for 45-60 minutes, or until they become tender and golden.

Meanwhile, cook the spelt by placing it in a large pan and covering it with salted water. Add the bay leaf and simmer gently over a medium heat for 30-35 minutes, until the spelt is soft yet still retains a bit of bite. Drain the cooked spelt thoroughly and transfer it to a large bowl.

Melt the butter in a frying pan. Once it is starting to foam a little, add the leeks and mushrooms and cook for 10 minutes, turning the heat down to a low medium. Season with salt, then add the garlic and cook for a further 2 minutes.

Add the drained spelt and chopped parsley to the frying pan, then crumble over the blue cheese. Stir to distribute evenly and then remove the pan from the heat.

Take the roasted squash out the oven and spoon the spelt mixture into them until each one is full. Put the tops on and return them to the oven for 8-10 minutes, then serve one whole stuffed squash per person. I love this with a good spoonful of soured cream on the side.

SKREI COD, MONK'S BEARD, JERUSALEM ARTICHOKE PURÉE, GOLDEN RAISIN DRESSING

SERVES 6

It's very easy to only consider seasonality when thinking about fruits and vegetables, as we can see it happen directly around us, but fish are also seasonal. No fish embodies this quite like the majestic skrei; a beautiful green-skinned, ice-white fleshed member of the cod family that has been sustainably fished in Norway for thousands of years. Every January, millions of skrei return to their Norwegian spawning grounds from deep in the Barents Sea; the icy swim and pure water create a delicate, lean meat. The only fish kept ashore are over five years old and a designated length and weight, ensuring the continuation of skrei for generations with minimal impact on the ecosystem, and the rest migrate back to the depths in March. Monk's beard, also known as agretti, is a delightful grassy herb which emerges in late winter: a fresh pop of greenery to brighten those dull months.

2 whole skrei cod loins

600ml almond milk

Sea salt

For the dressing

250g golden raisins

4 tbsp sherry vinegar

2 tsp wholegrain mustard

5 tsp capote capers

1 tsp caper brine

1 shallot, finely diced

½ lemon, juiced

½ tsp cumin seeds

250ml rapeseed oil

For the purée

500g Jerusalem artichokes

150ml double cream

For the monk's beard

50g unsalted butter

250g monk's beard, trimmed and washed

You can make the dressing a day ahead if you wish. Put the raisins and sherry vinegar into a pan, add enough water to cover and bring to the boil, then remove from the heat, cover and leave until cool. Add the mustard, capers and brine, shallot, lemon juice, and cumin seeds to the cooled raisin mixture, then pulse it in a food processor while adding the oil in a thin stream until emulsified. Store the dressing in an airtight container until needed.

Preheat your oven to 180°c. Place the Jerusalem artichokes in a roasting tin and wrap in tin foil. Bake for an hour until soft, then remove. Once cool enough to handle, slice them in half and scoop out the flesh into a saucepan. Place the skins back into the roasting tin, drizzle with rapeseed oil and season with salt, then bake for a further 20 minutes until crispy.

Add the cream to the pan of artichoke flesh with a good pinch of salt and heat gently, stirring to combine the two. Blitz with a stick blender and season to taste. Pass through a fine mesh sieve if you would like the purée silky smooth.

Wrap the skrei loins tightly in cling film and then cut them into 6 equal portions, leaving the cling film on. Pour the almond milk into a pan and bring to a simmer. Gently lower the skrei into the pan and poach for 8-10 minutes, until the flesh turns a beautiful pearl colour. If you have a kitchen probe, an internal temperature of 48°c is ideal to retain the moisture and allow the fish to flake naturally.

Finally, melt the butter for the monk's beard in a pan and add a splash of water. Add the monk's beard and cover with a lid, then cook for 1-2 minutes. Season with salt, drain and serve immediately alongside a spoonful of Jerusalem artichoke purée and the poached cod, removing the cling film from the fish. Drizzle the dressing around the dish and top with the crispy artichoke skins.

GRILLED HALIBUT, KERALAN STYLE MUSSEL CURRY SAUCE, CAULIFLOWER BHAJI

SERVES 4

Halibut is a rare treat today. Fished to the absolute brink in and around our waters, the world's largest flatfish must be left alone in the wild to recover. We used to source our restaurant halibut from an aquaculture farm on the Isle of Gigha in Scotland, which has sadly succumbed to the economic struggles we all face. Occasionally a good fishmonger will get their hands on Glitne halibut: sustainably farmed in Norway's Sognefjord and without doubt the best and most environmentally conscious halibut you can buy at the time of writing. Served here with a no waste cauliflower bhaji – the leaves are delicious – and a super punchy Keralan curry sauce enriched with mussels, this is a dish which celebrates halibut's majestic, pure flavour.

4 x 200g halibut portions
500ml brine (see page 249)

For the sauce
Rapeseed oil
1 onion, roughly chopped
1 small bunch of coriander stalks
1 tbsp garlic and ginger paste
1 tbsp smoked paprika
1 tbsp curry powder & ½ tsp ground cumin
2 tbsp tamarind paste
4 green cardamom pods
1 cinnamon stick & 2 star anise
6 dried curry leaves
400g mussels, cleaned and rinsed
2 tins of coconut milk
Sea salt

For the bhajis
1 cauliflower, florets and leaves thinly sliced
200g gram flour
1 tsp mild chilli powder
1 tsp ground turmeric & 1 tsp ground cumin
150-200ml sparkling water
1 lime, zested and juiced
Vegetable oil, for deep frying

To serve (optional)
450g white crab meat
150g cucumber relish (see page 256)

For the sauce

Heat a good splash of rapeseed oil in a large saucepan and fry the onion and coriander stalks until translucent. Add the garlic and ginger paste and cook for a further 2 minutes, then add the paprika, curry powder and cumin. Fry for 2 minutes, adding more oil if the pan gets too dry. Stir in the tamarind paste, cardamom, cinnamon, and star anise. Fry for 2-3 minutes until bubbling and thickening, then add the curry leaves and mussels. Cover with a lid and cook for 3 minutes, then remove the mussel shells and any unopened mussels, leaving the meat and mussel juice in the curry. Add the coconut milk and season with salt. Stir thoroughly to combine and simmer for 30 minutes. Remove the whole spices with a slotted spoon and set aside, then blitz the sauce with a stick blender until smooth. Press it through a mesh sieve into a clean pan, season to taste, add the whole spices back to the sauce and then simmer on a low heat for 20 minutes.

For the bhajis

Simmer the cauliflower florets and leaves in lightly salted water for 1-2 minutes until they begin to soften, then drain thoroughly and leave to cool completely. In a bowl, combine the gram flour, chilli powder, turmeric, cumin, and a pinch of salt. Gradually whisk in the sparkling water until a stiff batter forms (you may not need it all), then add the lime zest and juice, stirring until just combined. Gently fold in the cooled cauliflower until fully coated. Heat a pan one third full of the vegetable oil to 180°c (or until a cube of bread browns in 30 seconds). Carefully drop dessert spoons of bhaji batter into the hot oil, frying in batches for 3-4 minutes until crisp. Using a slotted spoon, transfer the bhajis to a plate lined with kitchen roll and season with salt.

Pour the brine over the halibut portions and leave for 15 minutes. Drain, rinse thoroughly and pat dry. Preheat your grill to its highest setting. Place the halibut portions on a suitable tray and drizzle with a little oil. Place under the grill for 8 minutes, then remove and turn over. Turn the grill off and place the fish back underneath until ready to serve.

Plate the halibut alongside the bhajis and sauce. The crab meat turned through the cucumber relish is a snappy addition which adds sweet heat but is entirely optional.

BRAISED PIG'S CHEEKS, TROTTER & PARSLEY CREAM, MUSTARD MASH, HONEY ROAST CHICORY

SERVES 6

I love the soft texture of pig's cheeks when slow cooked, but the real star here is the trotter sauce. It's so unctuous and rich, enhanced by parsley and cream to create a delicious classic sauce that you'll be finding excuses to make more and more of! This recipe uses the restaurant method for making mash which produces much more consistent results than boiling your spuds. Ask your butcher for pork rind when it comes to the crackling; there's always plenty spare and it's super cheap.

For the cheeks, sauce and crackling

18 pig's cheeks, trimmed of all fat and sinew

2.5 litres trotter stock (see page 249)

100ml double cream

1 bunch of curly parsley, chopped

250g pork rind, trimmed of all fat

Rapeseed oil

Sea salt

For the mash

2kg Rooster or Maris Piper potatoes, washed

200g unsalted butter

100ml double cream

50g wholegrain mustard

50g English mustard

For the chicory

3 heads of chicory, halved lengthways

1 tbsp runny honey

1 tbsp orange juice

1 tsp soy sauce

¼ tsp white miso paste

40g soft dark brown sugar

For the cheeks, sauce and crackling

Place the pig's cheeks in a large saucepan and pour over the trotter stock. Bring to a boil, then reduce the heat to a simmer and cover loosely with tin foil. Cook for 2 hours 30 minutes or until the pig's cheeks are soft to the touch. Remove the cheeks and set aside for later, then reduce the stock by half. Once reduced, add the cream and turn the heat down, then let the sauce simmer for 10 minutes. Set aside ready to finish with parsley just before serving.

Preheat your oven to 180°c. Using a sharp knife, cut the pork rind into long strips. Line a baking tray with parchment paper, and place the strips of rind on it, leaving space between each one. Liberally season with salt, drizzle with oil and top with another sheet of parchment, then press down with a similar size tray or tin. Place in the oven for 40 minutes until golden and crisp.

For the mash

Place the potatoes in a roasting tray and bake in the oven for 45 minutes, until the flesh feels soft. Once cool enough to handle, cut in half and spoon out the flesh. Heat the butter and cream in a large saucepan and pass the potato flesh through a sieve or potato ricer into the pan. Add the mustards and stir to combine evenly, seasoning with salt to taste.

For the chicory

Lay the chicory halves on a baking tray. Place the honey, orange juice, soy sauce, miso, and brown sugar in a saucepan and bring to a boil, stirring constantly to combine all the ingredients and form a syrupy viscosity. Drizzle this all over the chicory along with a little rapeseed oil, and roast in the oven for 30 minutes until the chicory is caramelised. Sprinkle with sea salt to taste.

To serve

Finish the sauce by adding the pig's cheeks to reheat them, then stirring in the chopped parsley 2 minutes before serving. Plate up alongside the mash and chicory, drizzling over the sauce and topping with a ribbon of crackling.

VENISON FAGGOTS, CELERIAC MASH, MUSHROOM, GHERKIN & GREEN PEPPERCORN SAUCE

SERVES 4

This is adapted from one of our winter classics which is served as a duo of venison with a seared loin (pictured) or venison rack. For me, the most enjoyable part of this plate is the spiced venison faggots, which have a rich gamey flavour that warms a weary winter soul. Celeriac, the poster boy of ugly-delicious vegetables, sings here with its peppery celery flavour, all rounded off with a piquant sauce of earthy mushrooms, spiky gherkins, and fiery green peppercorns. Caul fat will be available from a good local butcher, but I would recommend calling ahead to avoid disappointment. This a natural casing and really keeps the moisture and flavour in the faggots.

For the venison faggots

400g venison mince & 200g pork mince
120g chicken or venison livers, chopped
100g lardo, diced
50g prunes, chopped
2 cloves of garlic, grated
100g breadcrumbs
½ tsp ground white pepper
½ tsp smoked paprika
½ tsp ground nutmeg
300g caul fat
400ml chicken stock
Rapeseed oil

For the celeriac mash

500g Maris Piper or Rooster potatoes, peeled and diced
500g celeriac, peeled and diced
2 bay leaves
500ml milk
150g unsalted butter

For the sauce

400g flat mushrooms, thinly sliced
2 shallots, thinly sliced
2 gherkins, finely diced
2 sprigs of thyme
125ml red wine
500ml beef stock
40g green peppercorns
50g unsalted butter, cubed

For the venison faggots

Place the mince into a large mixing bowl, stir in the livers, lardo, prunes and garlic, then mix thoroughly with your hands. Add the breadcrumbs gradually, stopping as soon as the mixture is comfortably sticking together. Add the white pepper, paprika, and nutmeg with a good pinch of sea salt and mix thoroughly. Shape a small piece into a patty, pan fry until cooked through, taste and then adjust the seasoning accordingly.

Rinse the caul fat under running water for around 10 minutes. Squeeze dry and gently unroll into a large sheet. Shape the faggot mixture into balls and place along the caul fat, then trim the fat, leaving enough excess to ensure the faggots will be tightly wrapped. Wrap them in the caul and place in the fridge for 10 minutes. Pour the chicken stock into a large saucepan and bring to the boil, then reduce to a simmer. Heat a splash of rapeseed oil in a large frying pan on a medium heat and pan fry the faggots until browned all over (around 10 minutes), then transfer them into the chicken stock and simmer gently for a further 15 minutes. Remove and set aside.

For the celeriac mash

Place the potatoes, celeriac, bay leaves and milk into a large saucepan and season with salt. Cover with a cartouche of baking parchment and simmer until soft when touched with a knife. Drain the mixture, discarding the bay leaves but retaining the milk. Using the same pan, melt the butter and add the potatoes and celeriac back in. Begin to mash and gradually add the reserved milk until the desired consistency is reached. Season to taste.

For the sauce

Heat some rapeseed oil in a saucepan and gently cook the mushrooms and shallot for 10 minutes. Add the gherkins and thyme, cook for a further minute, add the red wine and bring to a rapid boil. Reduce by three quarters, add the beef stock and reduce by a third, then turn the heat down to a simmer and add the green peppercorns. Cook for a few minutes before adding the butter one cube at a time to help the sauce thicken. There will be more sauce here than you need but you can use the extra to reheat the faggots in, 15 minutes before serving.

Plate the reheated faggots on top of the mash, doused in the sauce. Use a slotted spoon to remove the mushrooms, shallot, gherkins and green peppercorns to finish the dish with.

ROAST BELLY PORK WITH FENNEL SEED CRACKLING

SERVES 4-6

Belly pork is both enriching and affordable but requires some cooking to get the meat beautifully soft. The reward for your patience is a delicious crisp crackling, taken out of the ordinary with a cracked spice infusion. Dipped in apple sauce, this is a hearty and wholesome roasting joint for colder days. Ask your butcher to score the skin for you, otherwise take extreme care to do so at home with a Stanley knife. The skin is thick and takes a firm hand to cut through, as you need to make sure you don't slice into the flesh below while going deep enough to allow the crackling to form.

3 tbsp fennel seeds

1 tbsp coriander seeds

1 tsp cumin seeds

1 tsp black peppercorns

1.5kg thick end of pork belly, skin scored

2 tbsp sea salt

Rapeseed or vegetable oil

Place the seeds and peppercorns into a pestle and mortar and coarsely grind until broken down but not powdered.

Place the pork belly in a roasting tin and season liberally with salt, then set aside for 1 hour. Once rested, scatter over the cracked seed mix and drizzle with plenty of oil. Ensure the seeds are pressed right into the score slices.

Preheat your oven to 220°c. Place the pork into the oven for 30 minutes, then turn the oven down to 180°c, leaving the pork in the oven. Continue roasting for 2 hours. If the crackling is still resisting the urge to pop, turn the heat back up to 200°c for 10 minutes.

Remove the pork from the oven and leave to rest uncovered for 20 minutes. To carve, carefully slide a knife between the crackling and the meat to remove it. Slice the meat into thick slices and cut the crackling separately to serve over the top.

TRUFFLE DAUPHINOISE, CARAMELISED ONION & LINCOLNSHIRE POACHER PIE

SERVES 8

This is a delicious vegetarian pie that takes all the good things we all love about a classic cheese and onion pie and turns the dial up to 11. Rich and creamy dauphinoise potato layered with luxury truffle flavour, topped with sweet sticky onions and a potent cheese? Absolute heaven. As with the other pie recipes in this book, the choice of pastry is entirely up to you, with recipes on page 250.

Butter, for greasing

500g pie pastry (I recommend shortcrust)

250g Lincolnshire Poacher, grated

2 egg yolks, beaten

For the truffle dauphinoise

500ml double cream

50ml black truffle oil

30g truffle paste

2 cloves of garlic, grated

3 sprigs of thyme, leaves only

1kg potatoes, peeled and thinly sliced

100g Gruyère cheese, grated

For the caramelised onions

Rapeseed oil

1kg onions, peeled and thinly sliced

Sea salt

For the truffle dauphinoise

For ease of assembly, I recommend making the dauphinoise the day before you want to serve the pie to allow the layers to set. Preheat your oven to 180°C. In a large saucepan, heat the cream, truffle oil and paste, garlic, and thyme leaves until just simmering. Season with salt to taste. Add the sliced potatoes and mix well.

Grease a roasting tin with a little butter and then pour in the potato mixture, pressing down to create an even spread. Sprinkle the grated Gruyère over the top and bake for 50-60 minutes or until the potatoes are tender and the top is golden brown. Remove and set aside to cool, then cover with parchment paper and place a weight on top. Leave in the fridge overnight to chill and set.

The following day, lightly grease a 20cm pie tin with butter and roll out your pastry to 3mm thickness. Lay the pastry into the tin, pressing it gently into the sides all the way around. Chill in the fridge for 30 minutes. Meanwhile, preheat your oven to 190°C and make the caramelised onions.

For the caramelised onions

Heat a little rapeseed oil in a large frying pan on a medium-high heat, then add the onions and fry until they turn a deep caramel colour, seasoning with salt about halfway through. Set aside.

To assemble the pie

Remove the dauphinoise from the fridge and turn it out of the roasting tin. Cut out a piece to fit perfectly inside the pie tin. Top with the caramelised onions and sprinkle over the Lincolnshire Poacher, then finish with a pie lid rolled out from the remaining pastry. Crimp the edges, then brush the beaten egg yolk over the lid with a pastry brush. Place in the oven and bake for 30 minutes.

VENISON WELLINGTON

SERVES 6

What a dish this turned out to be for us. Our first ever wellington was pork, and our regulars came back every week to try our tweaks and improvements to it. The time eventually came to take it off the menu, but the wellington dream never died, and in the Autumn of 2021 we brought it back, this time with venison loin. This wellington was the one eaten by Marina O'Loughlin during her visit to the pub, which she described as "unimprovable" in her Sunday Times review. We make it every year in the exact same way as a nod to the significance of that review and how much it helped our business.

800g venison loin

2 sprigs of thyme & 4 cloves of garlic

1 tbsp English mustard

1 onion & 400g flat mushrooms

8 slices of serrano ham

1 sheet of puff pastry

1 egg yolk

For the braised cabbage

½ a red cabbage

1 onion & 1 Bramley apple

250ml each of Port, red wine, red wine vinegar & balsamic vinegar

250g soft brown sugar

2 star anise, allspice berries & cloves

1 cinnamon stick

For the venison sauce

2 bay leaves & 2 sprigs of thyme

3 sticks of celery

1 carrot, onion and garlic bulb

1 tbsp redcurrant jelly

200ml Port & 500ml veal stock

For the chestnut purée

2 banana shallots

250g cooked chestnuts

50g butter

200ml double cream

2 sprigs of thyme

Trim any excess fat and sinew off the venison loin, setting the sinew aside for the sauce. Season the loin all over with salt. Add the thyme and garlic to a hot pan with some oil, then sear the venison loin on each side for 2 minutes. Set aside on a tray and brush with the English mustard. Finely dice the onion and flat mushrooms for the duxelles. Add oil to a pan and sweat off the onions and mushrooms, seasoning liberally with salt and cooking until as dry as possible. Set aside to cool. Lay a piece of cling film on the bench and spread out the ham slices evenly, slightly overlapping. Spread the mushroom duxelles over the ham to create an even layer. Place the venison loin in the centre, then roll the duxelles and ham around the loin using the cling film, tying it tightly at each end. Place in the fridge for half an hour.

For the braised cabbage

Very finely shred the red cabbage. Finely dice the onion, then peel and dice the apple, removing the core. Add all the ingredients for the braised cabbage to a large pan and cook on a medium heat until the liquid has reduced to a syrup, coating the cabbage. Stir regularly.

For the venison sauce

Brown off the reserved venison trim in a pan with the bay, thyme and some oil. Roughly dice the celery, carrot and onion, halve the garlic bulb and brown all the vegetables in the pan with the venison. Season with salt and stir in the redcurrant jelly, then add the Port. Reduce it by half, then add the veal stock and reduce by a quarter. Pass the sauce through a sieve into a clean pan and reduce by half, skimming any impurities from the top. Set aside and reheat when needed.

For the chestnut purée

Finely dice the shallots and add to a pan with the broken up chestnuts and butter. Sweat until golden, then add the cream and thyme. Bring to the boil, reduce to a simmer and cook for a further 5 minutes, then blitz until smooth and pass through a chinois. Reheat when ready to serve.

To cook the wellington, preheat your oven to 200°c. Unwrap the venison parcel from the cling film, and tightly wrap in the puff pastry. Brush with egg yolk and place on a baking tray in the oven for 20 minutes. To serve the wellington, cut either end off and then slice into even, round pieces. Serve alongside the chestnut purée, braised cabbage and venison sauce.

RED WINE POACHED PEARS, CINNAMON BUCKWHEAT CRUMB, CHANTILLY CREAM

SERVES 6

This is my particularly festive take on a classic poached pear, incorporating strong fragrant spices into a red wine based poaching liquor for a striking wintery pudding. Great pears are the key ingredient, and we're blessed in this country with some fine orchards growing heritage varieties that date back centuries. Williams pears are among my favourites, and their flesh is dry enough to withstand a lengthy poach, absorbing all the delicious liquid along the way. A nutty buckwheat crumb with cinnamon adds to the festive flavour, all cut through with a rich and indulgent Chantilly cream.

For the poached pears

750ml red wine

200g caster sugar

1 cinnamon stick

1 star anise

2 cloves

1 vanilla pod, split lengthways

6 Williams or Comice pears, peeled and cored

For the buckwheat crumb

100g buckwheat flour

50g unsalted butter, chilled and cubed

½ tsp ground cinnamon

For the Chantilly cream

300ml double cream

1 tsp vanilla paste

1 tsp icing sugar

In a large saucepan, combine the red wine with 150g of the caster sugar and the cinnamon stick, star anise, cloves, and vanilla pod. Bring to the boil, then reduce the heat and simmer for 5 minutes. Add the pears to the saucepan, making sure they are fully submerged in the liquid. Cover the saucepan with a lid and simmer for 30-45 minutes until the pears are tender.

While the pears are cooking, preheat your oven to 180°c. In a mixing bowl, combine the buckwheat flour, cubed butter, ground cinnamon and remaining 50g of caster sugar. Rub the ingredients together until they resemble coarse breadcrumbs. Spread this mixture out on a baking tray and bake in the preheated oven for 10-12 minutes until golden brown. Remove from the oven and allow to cool.

In a clean mixing bowl, whisk the double cream with the vanilla paste and icing sugar until it forms soft peaks and set aside in the fridge until ready to serve.

Once the pears are cooked, remove them from the saucepan and transfer to a serving dish. Bring the remaining poaching liquid to the boil and reduce by half to create a syrup.

To serve, place the buckwheat crumb on the plate with the poached pear on top, drizzled with the red wine syrup. Add a spoonful of Chantilly cream to the side and enjoy.

SALTED CARAMEL CUSTARD TART

SERVES 12

I remember my first time eating the original version of this at Adam Byatt's Trinity restaurant in Clapham in 2017, after which I set myself on a mission to recreate it almost immediately. It is testament to his original recipe that it took me about three years to get anywhere near it, and it was the greatest privilege when Adam himself declared our version to be worthy of the name. It's always on the menu, baked fresh every day. Get it first at lunch and it can still be slightly warm from the oven, which is a real treat.

For the pastry

350g plain flour
90g icing sugar
175g butter, cubed and chilled
1 egg
30ml water

For the custard

200ml egg yolk
120g caster sugar
14g Maldon sea salt
850ml double cream

For the caramel

150g caster sugar
40ml water

For the pastry

Combine the plain flour and icing sugar in the bowl of a stand mixer. Mix in the butter until the mixture resembles fine breadcrumbs. Add the egg and water and mix until combined. Turn off the mixer and tip the dough out onto a lightly floured work surface. Bring together so it has a smooth texture, then wrap in cling film and set in the fridge for 2 hours.

Preheat your oven to 170°c. Remove the pastry from the fridge and let it soften slightly. On a lightly floured surface, roll out the pastry to 3mm thickness. Lightly grease a 20cm tart tin and gently line it with the pastry, leaving 2cm hanging over the edge all the way round. Wrap a small spherical piece of dough in cling film and use it to press the pastry right into the edges of the tart tin. Gently top with greaseproof paper, fill with baking beans and leave to firm up in the fridge for 30 minutes.

Bake the pastry in the preheated oven for 20 minutes. Remove the baking beans and greaseproof paper, then shave the overhanging edges away with a vegetable peeler. Return to the oven and bake for a further 10 minutes, then set aside.

For the custard

Beat the egg yolk and caster sugar together in a mixing bowl. Add the salt and mix thoroughly. Pour the cream into a saucepan and bring to the boil. Once boiling, pour the cream over the egg and sugar mix while whisking, ensuring the mixture is thoroughly combined, then set aside.

For the caramel

Heat the sugar and water in a saucepan. Do not disturb the mix as it cooks, taking the temperature to 155°c. Once reached, carefully pour the caramel into the custard, whisking as you go until smooth. Skim the foam off the top and then pass the custard through a fine sieve into a jug.

Turn the oven temperature down to 130°c. Place the baked tart case in the oven and then pour in the salted caramel custard. Bake for 40 minutes, or until the tart is wobbly without looking runny underneath. Leave the tart on the side to cool to room temperature before cutting into 12 slices.

POACHED YORKSHIRE RHUBARB, GINGER CAKE, RHUBARB SYRUP

SERVES 4

The hot-pink spears of forced rhubarb – as sharp to taste as their colour suggests, grown by candlelight in long sheds scattered across the Rhubarb Triangle between Wakefield, Morley and Rothwell – provide a much-needed respite from the grey, earthy tones of Winter. Their arrival through our kitchen doors heralds an inkling of change, literally a light in the darkness as the first produce of the New Year, and a dream of Spring. I like to retain some of their inherent sharpness, and pairing them with a little fiery ginger cake makes for a delicious wintery afternoon tea.

For the poached rhubarb and syrup

2 litres water

1kg caster sugar

1kg Yorkshire forced rhubarb, cut into 4cm batons

For the ginger cake

375ml whole milk

165g soft dark brown sugar

165g golden syrup

150g unsalted butter

85g black treacle

80g ginger syrup

1 tsp bicarbonate of soda

300g self-raising flour

65g stem ginger, finely chopped

2 tbsp peeled and grated root ginger

1 tsp ground ginger

1 tsp mixed spice

1 egg, beaten

For the poached rhubarb and syrup

In a large saucepan, whisk the water and sugar together until combined. Place on a high heat and allow the sugar to dissolve, then bring to a rapid boil. Take off the heat and add the rhubarb batons, ensuring they are fully submerged in the syrup.

Cover and set aside for 30 minutes until the rhubarb is soft, then remove it from the syrup and place in an airtight container in the fridge. Retain the syrup, placing it back onto the heat to reduce by half, then set aside in a heatproof container until ready to serve.

For the ginger cake

Place the milk and brown sugar in a pan and bring to the boil. At the same time in a separate pan, gently heat the golden syrup, butter, treacle, and ginger syrup until fully combined. Remove from the heat and whisk in the bicarbonate of soda. Allow this and the milk mixture to cool to room temperature.

Preheat your oven to 160°c and line a 16cm cake tin or standard loaf tin with baking parchment. Sift the flour into a large mixing bowl and add all three types of ginger along with the mixed spice, stirring to combine evenly. Slowly pour in the sweetened milk and mix to combine, then repeat with the butter and syrup mixture. Finally, stir in the beaten egg until you have a smooth paste.

Transfer the mixture to the cake tin and bake for 50 minutes, then remove from the oven and place the tin onto a wire rack. Let it cool to room temperature before you cut the cake into slices to match the size of the rhubarb batons.

To serve

Place the poached rhubarb on top of the sliced ginger cake and drizzle over the rhubarb syrup.

DARK CHOCOLATE MOUSSE, STOUT CAKE, MILK ICE CREAM

SERVES 6

A lovely dessert to make if you have plenty of time to get organised for it, as this needs to be done at least a day ahead. The use of dark chocolate and iron-rich stout cake add a wintery bitterness to this dessert which is beautifully balanced by the super-rich condensed milk ice cream. The mousse recipe was honed by Paul, our executive chef, whose repertoire and skill interlink perfectly with my vision and bring it to life.

For the ice cream

300ml double cream
200ml whole milk
100ml condensed milk
100g caster sugar
3 egg yolks (60ml)

For the mousse

375ml whipping cream
175g caster sugar
25ml water
3g sea salt
100ml double cream
175g good quality dark chocolate
2 sheets of bronze leaf gelatine
5 egg yolks (100ml)

For the cake

250g unsalted butter, softened
400g soft dark brown sugar
2 eggs, beaten
250g self-raising flour
80g cocoa powder
150g Greek yoghurt
250ml stout

A day before serving, make all the elements for this dish, starting with the ice cream.

For the ice cream

Add the cream and both milks to a pan and bring to the boil. In a mixing bowl, beat the sugar and egg yolks together. Pour the boiling cream into this mixture, whisking continuously. Pour back into the pan and heat to precisely 82°c, then pour into a suitable container with a lid. Leave to cool overnight, churn in the ice cream machine first thing in the morning, then transfer to the freezer.

For the mousse

Pour the whipping cream into a large mixing bowl and whip until stiff, then set aside. Place the sugar and water in a pan on a medium heat and cook to a light golden caramel, then add the sea salt and double cream. Half fill another saucepan with water and bring it to the boil. Reduce to a simmer and place a glass or metal mixing bowl over the top. Melt the chocolate in the bowl, stirring occasionally.

Meanwhile, soak the gelatine leaves in a little water for a few minutes, then remove and squeeze out any excess water. Add the gelatine to the melted chocolate along with the egg yolks and your salted caramel. Add this mixture to the whipped cream, folding gently until combined, then divide the mousse evenly between 6 bowls. Place in the fridge overnight to set.

For the cake

Preheat your oven to 160°c and line a 20cm cake tin with baking parchment. In a mixing bowl, cream together the butter and sugar, then add the eggs. Sift in the flour and cocoa powder, mix to combine, and finally fold through the yoghurt and stout until smooth. Pour the mix into the cake tin and bake for 30 minutes, then transfer to a cooling rack before slicing into cubes. Store in an airtight container.

To serve

Smooth over the tops of the set mousse with the back of a hot spoon an hour before serving. Top with cubes of stout cake and scoops of ice cream.

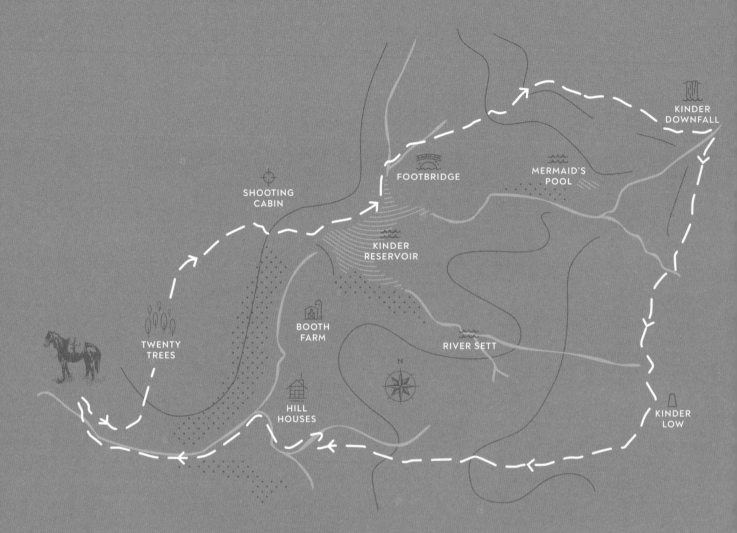

Kinder Downfall

8½ MILES, STRENUOUS, 636M SUMMIT, ALLOW 5 HOURS.

This walk is not for the inexperienced or ill-equipped: it includes long, steep climbs and descents over rough and rocky moorland terrain. Walking boots and Ordnance Survey map OL1 recommended. Pack food and waterproofs and do not attempt in bad weather. If you get into difficulty, become lost, or lose daylight, contact Mountain Rescue immediately by calling 999, ask for the police, and then Mountain Rescue. Likely to be boggy or muddy in places; several streams to ford.

This is a dramatic and strenuous walk to Kinder Downfall, the highest waterfall in the Peak District. In high winds the falling waters are blown uphill by the funnelling effect of the valley below. In hard winters, the waterfall freezes and presents a spectacular sight as well as a rare and irresistible challenge to ice climbers. On a clear day, magnificent views are afforded from the summit all the way to the mountains of Snowdonia some 90 miles away in Wales. Other notable scenery on offer includes an excellent view of Greater Manchester, Pendle Hill, Pen-Y-Ghent, and the extensive, seemingly endless, rolling hills of the Derbyshire Dark Peak.

From the front door of The Pack Horse, turn left. Bear right over the River Sett and keep left of the church up the main road, Church Street, passing The George Hotel and the fish and chip shop. At the top of Church Street, turn left and left again into Valley Road.

Follow Valley Road, keeping left following the river, but not crossing it. After a row of terraced houses on the right, the path descends to a no-through road. Keep left again at the fork bearing the owl carving, keeping the high stone retaining wall on your right. Descend to the river and after the last houses, follow the riverside path, ignoring a footbridge. When the path divides, keep left through the gateposts and walk between the river and the campsite. Keep an eye out for the heron.

Follow to the end of the road and at the campsite entrance, go straight on along the metalled road to the right of the stream. Follow the road to the right at the confluence of the Sett and Kinder rivers, which offers views ahead to Bowden pack horse bridge just as you turn the corner. The road crosses the river on a bridge below a small weir. At a crossroads, go straight on through the gateposts and follow the track uphill. Follow the road round to the right as it crosses the stream to reach Tunstead House, which the path skirts via a track on your right. Beyond the buildings, follow a short, walled section to reach open fields. Keep along the left-hand wall of the first field, then cross the middle of the next three fields, heading relentlessly uphill from gate to gate. In the fifth field, as the slope eases off, keep parallel to the right-hand wall until you reach a gateway and then a further gate into open country by the scattered remains of a ruined building

Turn left briefly across rushy ground to the higher of two gates, then turn immediately right, steeply up the spine of Kinder Low End ridge. The steepest central section is pitched with stones. Beyond the rocky section the gradient eases, but the path continues uphill along the centre of the ridge to a further rocky outcrop. Pick up the paved path that skirts to the right of Kinder Low Bowl Barrow. Keep left when another paved path joins from the right, following the slabs to the trig point on Kinder Low. At the trig point, turn left to reach the plateau edge at a cairn. Follow the edge path for a little over a mile to Kinder Downfall, fording Red Brook above its rocky valley about halfway along. At times, particularly in the rockier sections, there is a choice of paths and the way forward is indistinct, but route-finding is generally simple: keep between the peat on your right and the steeper ground dropping away to your left.

Ford the shallow River Kinder above the Downfall and continue along the plateau edge in similar fashion to before, except now heading northwest. After a little under a mile, having climbed to a minor rocky summit followed by a level stretch with sandy sections, the path reaches a projecting spur of land where the edge path turns sharp right. Turn left here and leave the Kinder Scout plateau, descending fairly steeply down the grassy shoulder.

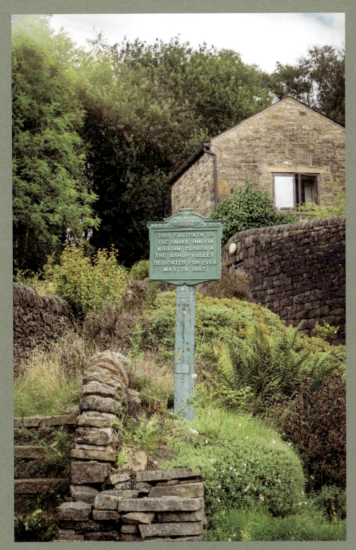

Towards the bottom you ford a small stream, then descend further to cross the footbridge over William Clough, just above the head of the reservoir. Turn left and follow the path above and along the reservoir wall. At a fork, take the right-hand (upper) path that climbs slightly through the heather, leading away from the reservoir. Rejoin the reservoir wall at a hand-gate and continue along the wall, below open woodland. After an information board erected to mark the centenary of the reservoir, level with the dam, turn right, uphill. Follow the path alongside the wall to a gate at the top. Bear left then right across the open moor to a junction of paths below the shooting cabin. Turn left (signposted "Hayfield 1½ miles"). Follow the obvious path through the heather to a National Trust sign for the Snake Path. Go through the kissing gate and follow the track across rough grazing land.

After a stretch alongside a wall, go through a gate and cross the field, aiming for the treetops of Twenty Trees. Follow the wall and then go through a kissing gate on your right, above the clump of trees. Bear left past the trees to a further kissing gate and commemorative sign. Descend along the bottom of the next field to a gate and stile. Follow the track beyond, which bends left to join a concrete drive and leads down to Kinder Road. Turn right and walk downhill past the library. At the junction with Bank Street, continue ahead along Kinder Road back to The Pack Horse.

PERFECT ROAST POTATOES

SERVES 6

A 50/50 ratio of oil and fat is the key to success here. Avoid extra virgin olive oil as its flavour taints when cooked and it has a very low smoke point. Steaming the potatoes prior to roasting is a must for those crispy edges and fluffy centres. Choosing the right potato is essential; something floury like King Edward or Maris Piper is great. We use Roosters at the pub, and the heritage variety Arran Victory when in season.

1.5kg floury potatoes, peeled and chopped

75ml rapeseed or vegetable oil

75g duck fat (or beef or lamb fat depending on your meat joint)

1 bulb of garlic, broken into cloves with the skin on

4 sprigs of thyme

Sea salt, to taste

Preheat your oven to 190°c. Place the potatoes into a steamer for 18 minutes. Tip into a colander and, without fluffing too much, let them dry out completely.

Put the oil and fat into a large roasting tin and place in the oven for 5 minutes. Remove, and carefully tip the potatoes into the hot fat. Season liberally with salt, scatter over the garlic cloves and thyme, then gently turn the potatoes in the tray. Make sure to leave as much space as you can between the potatoes – the more the air can circulate, the crispier they get.

Place in the oven for 25-40 minutes depending on how you like your roasties cooked, turning the potatoes halfway through. Don't discard the garlic cloves at the end, they're ridiculously tasty.

SUNDAY GRAVY BASE

MAKES APPROX. 1 LITRE

This is time consuming, but worth the end result. I've adapted this from the recipe we use in the pub, as that gravy takes 3 days to reduce properly which isn't practical at home. This is the same base and produces excellent results in a quarter of the time. I've named it a gravy base as it's great to have on hand and is always enhanced by the addition of any roasting juices prior to serving.

Rapeseed oil

2 carrots, peeled and roughly diced

1 large onion, peeled and roughly diced

50ml red wine vinegar

2 sticks of celery, roughly diced

1 bulb of garlic, halved

2 sprigs of thyme

2 bay leaves

50g redcurrant jelly

750ml red wine

3 litres good quality beef stock

1 tbsp beef gravy granules

Sea salt, to taste

Heat some rapeseed oil in a large saucepan and once hot, add the carrots. Fry them intensely until caramelised all over, then set aside and repeat with the onion. Remove the onion and deglaze the pan by adding the red wine vinegar, letting it reduce right down to a syrup, then pour it over the caramelised vegetables.

Give the pan a wipe and reset it with oil over a medium heat. Add the celery, garlic, thyme and bay, plus the caramelised vegetable mixture, and cook for 10 minutes, stirring occasionally. Season with salt, then add the redcurrant jelly and the bottle of wine, turning the heat right up to boil away the alcohol. Leave on a high heat and reduce the wine until only a quarter remains. Add the beef stock 1 litre at a time, reducing by half before adding the next.

Once the final litre has been fully incorporated and reduced, pass the gravy into a fresh pan using a sieve to strain off all the vegetables, then whisk in the beef gravy granules and bring to the boil one last time, whisking for a further 5 minutes. You can add more gravy granules should you want a thicker gravy. Adjust the seasoning to taste and serve when ready.

YORKSHIRE PUDDINGS

SERVES 6

Low-stress, low-maintenance Yorkshire puddings should exist in every kitchen. Which is the exact opposite of the experience I had in our early days. Inexperienced and unable to master an unruly gas oven, I refused to serve any Yorkshire puddings during our first few Sundays, embarrassed at my failed attempts. The recipe evolved as my knowledge grew, and life became much, much easier.

5 eggs
500ml whole milk
4g sea salt
250g plain flour
Vegetable oil

Yorkshire pudding batter is best made the night before, but at the very least do it 2 hours before baking. Break the eggs into a large mixing bowl, pour over the milk and add the salt, then sift in the flour. Whisk together, removing the lumps. Cover and place in the fridge.

Preheat your oven to 180°c. Remove the batter from the fridge and carefully skim off the layer of foam developing on the top. Take a non-stick deep muffin tin and cover the bottom of each hole with oil. Place in the oven until the oil is smoking. Carefully pour the batter into each hole evenly, until around two thirds full. Place in the oven and leave totally undisturbed for 35 minutes, then remove and serve straight away.

CARROT & SWEDE MASH

SERVES 6

Something of a signature on our Pack Horse roasts; I can't live without this on Sundays now. You can be generous with the black pepper, swede loves it.

1 swede, peeled and diced
2 carrots, peeled and diced
250g butter
1 onion, peeled and diced
2 cloves of garlic, peeled and grated
100ml double cream, plus extra to hand
Sea salt and cracked black pepper, to taste

Bring a large pan of salted water to the boil and add the diced swede and carrot. Boil for 30 minutes, or until totally soft and yielding. Empty into a colander and leave to dry. Using the same pan, add half the butter and once melted, add the diced onion. Gently sweat until translucent, then add the grated garlic and cook for a further 5 minutes. Add the rest of the butter, the cream and the cooked carrot and swede, then blitz with a stick blender until mash-like, adding more cream if you want a looser consistency. Season with salt and pepper to taste.

HONEY ROAST ROOTS

SERVES 6

A Sunday classic: delicious, simple, and easy to fit around the timings of your meat and potatoes.

2 large parsnips

2 large carrots

1 celeriac

Rapeseed oil

10 sprigs of thyme, leaves only

3 tbsp runny honey

Peel the parsnips and carrots, top and tail them, slice in half lengthways and then once across to cut them into quarters. Peel the celeriac and take the thick root off the bottom, then cut into wedges the same size as the carrots and parsnips. Toss the roots in a roasting tin with the rapeseed oil and thyme leaves, then drizzle over the runny honey. Place in a preheated oven at 190°c for 30 minutes.

ROAST SAVOY CABBAGE & CARAWAY BUTTER

SERVES 6

Cabbage is a brute of a vegetable. Treat it as such with big flavour combinations and some robust cooking and it will reward you.

1 large savoy cabbage

2 tbsp caraway seeds

2 cloves of garlic, peeled

250g butter

Rapeseed or vegetable oil

Sea salt, to taste

Remove the outer leaves from the cabbage and cut into 6 equal wedges. Place the caraway seeds in a pestle and mortar and grind to a cracked consistency. Finely slice the garlic cloves. Heat a large heavy-based frying pan on the hob with a splash of oil, then add the cabbage wedges. Once the cabbage begins to colour, turn the wedges, and add the butter and caraway. Fry for a further 3 minutes and baste the cabbage in the butter, spooning it all over until covered. Add the garlic slices and salt, baste once more, then turn so the coloured side is facing up. Transfer to a preheated oven at 180°c and roast for 10 minutes. Remove and serve smothered in the caraway butter.

CREAMED SPINACH

SERVES 6

I normally bring this one out at Christmas as it's a bit of a showstopper, inspired by many a bowl consumed at Hawksmoor. It may be the greatest vegetable side dish in the world.

1kg fresh spinach

600ml double cream

2 large sprigs of thyme

4 cloves of garlic, crushed and chopped

1 tsp freshly grated nutmeg

¼ tsp cayenne pepper

Sea salt and cracked black pepper, to taste

Heat a pan of salted water on the hob. Once boiling, add the first batch of spinach and blanch for 1-2 minutes, then remove with a slotted spoon and refresh in iced water immediately. Repeat this process until all the spinach is cooked. Drain the spinach and squeeze as much moisture from it as you can, then chop it up. Place the cream, thyme, garlic, nutmeg, and cayenne in a pan. Bring to a simmer, then remove from the heat and leave to infuse for 2 hours. Mix the cooled, infused cream into the spinach, season to taste with salt and pepper, then reheat when required.

CAULIFLOWER CHEESE

SERVES 6-8

Surely the nation's favourite Sunday side: it would be silly not to include our version of this. The cheese sauce is the key and great cheese makes all the difference. Don't be alarmed by the inclusion of blue cheese; it really works, and you'll find it adds something unique to the sauce rather than just dominating it.

2 cauliflowers, cut into florets

125g butter

125g plain flour

1.5 litres whole milk

1 tsp freshly grated nutmeg

1½ tsp ground white pepper

1½ tsp garlic powder

250g Lincolnshire Poacher

100g Colston Bassett Stilton

100g mozzarella

50g Ogleshield

100g Lord of the Hundreds, or parmesan

Sea salt, to taste

A handful of chopped chives

Preheat your oven to 200°c. Bring a pan of salted water to the boil and add the cauliflower florets. Boil for 6 minutes until just softening, then drain and set aside.

In a large saucepan, melt the butter over a low heat. Once melted, add the flour and cook through for around 3 minutes. Gradually add the milk, whisking as you go. Bring to a gentle boil, then reduce to a simmer, making sure it doesn't catch or start to burn on the bottom of the pan (you will need to start again if this happens). Whisk in the nutmeg, white pepper and garlic powder.

Grate or crumble all the cheeses separately and gradually add them to the sauce one by one, except the Lord of the Hundreds. Stir to combine and allow the cheese to thoroughly melt into the sauce, then season to taste with salt.

Add the cooked cauliflower and turn it through the sauce, then spoon everything into a roasting tin and top with the Lord of the Hundreds. Bake in the preheated oven for 20 minutes or until caramelised on top, then finish with the chopped chives.

CHICKEN STOCK

Makes 2 litres

1kg chicken bones or carcass
1 onion, roughly chopped
2 carrots, roughly chopped
2 sticks of celery, roughly chopped
4 cloves of garlic, smashed
1 lemon, halved
1 bay leaf
1 tsp black peppercorns
4 litres cold water
Sea salt, to taste

Preheat your oven to 200°c. Roast the chicken bones or carcass in a roasting tin for about 30 minutes, or until browned, then transfer to a large pot. Add the onion, carrot, celery, garlic, lemon, bay leaf, peppercorns, and enough water to cover all the ingredients. Bring to the boil over a high heat, then reduce to a low heat and simmer for 3-4 hours, or until the stock has reduced by half, skimming off any foam or impurities that rise to the surface of the stock as you go. Remove from the heat and strain through a fine-mesh strainer into a clean pot or container. Season to taste with salt. Once cooled, pour into suitable airtight containers. It will last in the freezer for a month.

BEEF STOCK

Makes 2 litres

2kg beef bones
1 onion, roughly chopped
2 carrots, roughly chopped
2 sticks of celery, roughly chopped
1 bulb of garlic, halved horizontally
2 bay leaves
1 tsp black peppercorns
4 litres cold water
Sea salt, to taste

Preheat your oven to 200°c. Place the beef bones on a baking tray and roast in the oven for 30 minutes until browned, turning occasionally, then transfer to a large stockpot. Add the onion, carrot, celery, garlic, bay leaves, and peppercorns. Pour in the cold water and bring to the boil over a high heat. Once boiling, reduce the heat and let it simmer for 6-8 hours, skimming the surface occasionally to remove any impurities. Strain the stock through a fine-mesh strainer into a large bowl or container. Season to taste with salt. Discard the solids. Let the stock cool to room temperature, then transfer it to an airtight container and store in the fridge for up to 5 days. Alternatively, freeze the stock for up to 3 months.

VEGETABLE STOCK

Makes 2 litres

1 tbsp rapeseed oil
2 onions, roughly chopped
2 leeks, roughly chopped
2 carrots, roughly chopped
2 sticks of celery, roughly chopped
1 bulb of garlic, halved horizontally
2 bay leaves
2 sprigs of thyme
1 tsp black peppercorns
4 litres cold water

Heat the oil in a large stockpot over medium heat. Add the onion, leek, carrot, and celery, and cook for 5-7 minutes until the vegetables are softened and starting to colour. Add the garlic, bay leaves, thyme, and peppercorns, then cook for an additional 2-3 minutes. Pour in the water and bring to the boil, then reduce the heat to low and let it simmer for 1-2 hours. Strain the stock through a fine-mesh strainer into a large bowl or container. Discard the solids. Leave to cool to room temperature, then transfer to an airtight container and store in the fridge for up to 5 days. Alternatively, you can freeze the stock for up to 3 months.

FISH STOCK

Makes 2 litres

1kg fish bones (such as cod, halibut, or sole)
2 onions, chopped
2 carrots, chopped
2 sticks of celery, chopped
2 cloves of garlic, smashed
2 bay leaves
2 star anise
1 clove
1 tsp black peppercorns
4 litres cold water

Rinse the fish bones under cold running water and place them in a large stockpot. Add the onion, carrot, celery, garlic, bay leaves, star anise, clove, and peppercorns to the pot, then cover with the water. Bring to the boil over a high heat, then reduce the heat and simmer for 45-60 minutes. Strain the stock through a fine-mesh strainer into a large bowl or container. Discard the solids. Let the stock cool to room temperature, then transfer it to an airtight container and store in the fridge for up to 5 days. Alternatively, you can freeze the stock for up to 1 month.

TROTTER STOCK

Makes 2 litres

4 pig's trotters, torched of all hair
2 sticks of celery, peeled and halved
1 large onion, peeled and halved
1 carrot, peeled and halved
1 leek, split in half
1 bulb of garlic, halved
1 sprig of thyme
1 bay leaf
4 black peppercorns
3 litres chicken stock
250ml Madeira

Put all the ingredients in a large stockpot and bring to the boil, then reduce the heat and simmer for 3-4 hours. Strain the liquor into a new pan, discard the vegetables and set the trotters aside. Once cool enough to handle, pick all the trotter meat, skin and sinew off the bones and add this back to the liquor. Cook for a further 30 minutes. Set aside and leave to cool, then transfer the stock to an airtight container and store in the fridge for up to 5 days. Alternatively, you can freeze the stock for up to 3 months.

PICKLING LIQUOR & BRINE

For the pickling liquor (makes 1 litre)
500ml white wine vinegar
500ml water
250g caster sugar

For the brine (makes 3 litres)
300g fine salt
200g caster sugar
6 juniper berries
6 black peppercorns
4 cloves
2 bay leaves
2 litres water

Place all the ingredients in a large pan and bring to the boil. Make sure all the sugar and salt has thoroughly dissolved, then reduce the heat and simmer for 10 minutes. Leave to cool, then store in an airtight container for up to 3 months.

CLASSIC SHORTCRUST

A great introductory pastry which is both simple and forgiving.
It makes a delicious whole pie with a slightly drier filling.

250g plain flour
A pinch of sea salt
125g unsalted butter, diced and chilled
1-3 tbsp cold water

Sift the flour and salt into a mixing bowl, add the diced butter and rub together with your fingertips until the mixture resembles breadcrumbs. Add the water gradually, as you may not need it all, starting with 1 tablespoon. Add more water gradually until the mixture comes together to form a firm, dry dough. Shape the dough into a disc, wrap in cling film and store in the fridge until needed.

PUFF PASTRY

Making puff pastry is a laborious task but it rewards you eventually with those beautiful layered flakes of buttery lightness. A perfect topper for a pot pie, though I know some of you will say that's just a casserole with a lid, but hey, what's not to love?

200g plain flour
A pinch of sea salt
100g unsalted butter, diced and chilled
100ml iced water

Sift the flour and salt into the bowl of a stand mixer. Add the cubed butter and begin to mix on a low speed, slowly trickling in the water to bring everything together to a firm dough. You may not need to use all the water. Lightly flour a work surface and shape the pastry into a rectangle. Roll out the pastry into a long rectangle approximately 1cm thick. To create the puffy layers, take the top third of the pastry and fold into the centre, then repeat with the bottom third to form a layered pastry block. Turn the pastry 90 degrees and repeat the whole rolling and folding process a further 7 times. Wrap the folded block of pastry in cling film and chill in the fridge for 30 minutes before rolling out to use.

HOT WATER PASTRY

This is a more technical pastry that creates a rich and incredibly strong case, perfect for wet fillings and traditional pork pies. I have to thank Stosie Madi at Parkers Arms for introducing me to this; she is the queen of pies and an extremely talented chef running a wonderful pub.

300g plain flour
10g sea salt
200g lard
100ml water
1 egg yolk

Sift the flour and salt into a mixing bowl. In a pan, gently heat the lard and water until the lard has melted and the water is warm. Pour this over the flour and mix, finally adding the egg yolk. Plan ahead with this as you will need to work while the mixture is warm; this pastry is incredibly firm once cooled. Have your filling ready and your pie tin ready to line, then cut the lid out, fill and crimp. It can then be left to firm up and chill for 30 minutes before baking.

PASTA DOUGH

Simple, delicious, generous: making fresh pasta dough is the most rewarding thing and once you've tried it, you'll be doing it all the time. It takes time and care but having a few portions of this family-size dough recipe in your freezer will transform what you can do for dinner parties, from simple lasagne sheets all the way up to artistic filled pastas. It blows the egg-free supermarket stuff away: this is proper pasta, as the Italians should force on us.

300g good-quality 00 grade flour, plus extra for dusting

50g fine semolina

9 egg yolks

3 tbsp cold water

2 tbsp extra virgin olive oil

On a clean work surface, make a mountainous pile of the flour and semolina combined, then make a well in the centre. Add the egg yolks to the well along with the cold water and olive oil. Using a fork, whisk the yolks until smooth and gradually bring the flour into the centre, whisking until you have to use your hands. Bring the dough together and knead for about 3-4 minutes until smooth, dusting with a little extra flour if needed. Wrap in cling film and leave to relax for 30 minutes.

Set up your pasta machine. Divide the pasta dough into quarters and begin to pass them through the machine on its thickest setting. Do this about 3 times so it is smooth and even, then reduce the thickness setting and repeat, all the way down to the thinnest setting. Cut into your desired shapes: 2mm wide strips for linguini, 8mm for tagliatelle, and 24mm for pappardelle.

ROSEMARY & SEA SALT FOCACCIA

Our signature bread that's served to all our guests, this focaccia recipe is easy, forgiving, and tasty. A perfect bread for beginners to master, and one we are really proud of. Definitely best enjoyed on the same day you bake it.

350g strong white bread flour

7g fast-acting dried yeast

9g cooking salt

230ml water

50ml good quality olive oil

4 sprigs of rosemary, leaves only

Flaky sea salt

Combine the flour and yeast in a mixing bowl, then add the cooking salt. Mix while gradually adding the water, then knead until the dough becomes smooth and elastic. This normally takes around 10 minutes. Line a large roasting tray with baking parchment, then place the dough in the tray and prove overnight in the fridge, covered with cling film. Alternatively, leave to prove on the side for 2 hours. Take the tray out of the fridge 1 hour before baking and poke dimples into the top. Coat with the olive oil, then throw over the rosemary leaves and sea salt flakes. Bake in the oven at 210°c for 25 minutes, then cool on a wire rack before serving.

SODA BREAD

This yeast-free bread is another great introduction to the world of bread making, and features on our menus throughout the year. It is my bread of choice to have with poached eggs and hollandaise in the morning.

300ml buttermilk

100ml whole milk

50g black treacle

25g unsalted butter

300g wholemeal flour

50g porridge oats

1 tbsp bicarbonate of soda

Sea salt

Lightly grease a standard loaf tin with a little unsalted butter. Combine the buttermilk and milk in a mixing bowl and bring up to room temperature. In a pan, melt the treacle and butter together, then allow to cool. Pour the treacle mix into the buttermilk mix and then add the flour, oats, bicarbonate of soda, and a good pinch of sea salt. Stir to form a wet, rough dough. Place the dough into the loaf tin and bake at 185°c for 25 minutes. Remove from the tin, place on a baking tray and bake for a further 15 minutes, then cool on a wire rack before serving.

ONION BHAJI

MAKES 12

Is this the nation's favourite curry side dish? If you have the facilities to make your own at home, they can very easily be much better than your local takeaway's version. Perfect for dipping in mint yoghurt as a pre-curry snack.

100g gram flour
1 tsp baking powder
1 tsp curry powder
¼ tsp cayenne pepper
100ml cold water
2 onions, finely sliced
1 green chilli, deseeded and very finely chopped
Vegetable oil for frying

In a mixing bowl, combine the gram flour, baking powder, curry powder, and cayenne pepper. Slowly add the cold water while whisking to create a thick batter. Add the onion and chilli to the mix, stirring to ensure they are fully coated.

Pour around 5cm of oil into a high sided pan (but do not fill the pan by more than a third) and place on a medium heat. Add a drop of batter to test whether the oil is ready; the batter should sizzle and skim the surface on impact. Spoon the bhaji mix into the hot oil, leaving to cook for 2 minutes before turning and cooking for a further 2 minutes. You may need to do this in batches so the pan doesn't become too crowded. Once all the bhajis are cooked, take the pan off the heat, remove the bhajis with a slotted spoon and drain them on a piece of kitchen roll. Serve warm.

MINT YOGHURT

SERVES 8

A perfect accompaniment for a spicy curry, and great to have on the table for those partial to dipping their poppadoms.

450ml natural yoghurt
1 bunch of mint, leaves only
½ bunch of coriander, leaves only
1 clove of garlic, peeled
Zest of 1 lime
A pinch of sea salt

Place all the ingredients into a food processor and blitz together. Portion into ramekins and serve.

KACHUMBER

SERVES 6

This is a lovely fresh salad which pairs beautifully with drier curries and is a great table salad in the summer months, as well as a topping for flatbreads.

1 cucumber, deseeded and cubed

4 tomatoes, deseeded and diced

1 red onion, finely diced

Approximately 40 coriander leaves, chopped

Juice and zest of 1 lime

1 tsp cumin seeds

A pinch of sea salt

Place all the ingredients into a mixing bowl, stir together and then leave to one side for 20 minutes before serving. The salt will draw out the moisture from the salad, creating a delicious cumin-flavoured dressing. Stir the salad once more before serving.

ONION SEED FLATBREAD

SERVES 8

I love the simplicity of this quick yeast-free bread. It's a great substitute at home for Indian breads, and it's what we serve at the pub with every curry on a Wednesday. Great for mopping up sauces, and ideal for barbecues to wrap grilled meats in too.

250g plain flour

1 tsp fine sea salt

1 tbsp black onion seeds

1 tbsp rapeseed oil

150ml warm water

Sift the flour and salt into a bowl along with the onion seeds. Add the oil to the warm water, then pour this over the flour in a thin stream, mixing with your hands to form a sticky dough. Lightly flour a work surface and turn the dough out onto it, kneading for around 5 minutes until it feels smooth.

Place the dough in a mixing bowl and cover with cling film, then leave to rest for 20 minutes. Roll the rested dough into a log and cut into 8 equal pieces. Flour the worktop again and roll out the pieces into thin circles approximately 2mm thick. Be generous with the flour if they start to stick.

Heat a non-stick frying pan on a high heat. When the pan is just at the point of smoking, turn the heat down to medium-high and add the first flatbread. Cook on one side for 1-2 minutes until the dough starts to lift away from the pan, then flip and cook the second side for 45 seconds. You're looking for some nicely charred bits on the dough, and if you like this simply fry them for longer. Place the cooked flatbread on a plate lined with a tea towel and wrap them up in the towel as you cook the rest. These are best served still warm.

TOMATO KETCHUP

MAKES ROUGHLY 1 LITRE

Our house ketchup recipe makes all branded ketchup look very average indeed. Complex, spicy and sweet, once you make this you'll never go back to supermarket ketchup. Best of all, it keeps in the fridge for about a month.

2 cloves

2 star anise

3 black peppercorns

3 whole allspice berries

1 large onion, peeled and roughly chopped

300g Bramley apples, peeled, cored and diced

650g fresh tomatoes, diced (preferably San Marzano)

250ml distilled malt vinegar

200g tomato paste

200g caster sugar

1 tsp sea salt

180ml shop-bought tomato ketchup

Place the cloves, star anise, black peppercorns, and allspice berries in a piece of muslin cloth and tie the top to form a spice bag. Heat some oil in a large pan and gently sweat the onion and apple until soft and translucent, then add the fresh tomatoes, malt vinegar, tomato paste, sugar, and salt. Bring to the boil, then reduce the heat to low and simmer for 2-3 hours. Take the pan off the heat and stir in the shop-bought ketchup. Remove the spice bag, then pass the ketchup through a sieve into an airtight container and store in the fridge for up to 1 month.

MAYONNAISE

MAKES 500ML

Another favourite condiment that we make in-house for all our guests, this mayonnaise is how I imagine mayo used to taste decades ago. It punches well above the heavily diluted branded versions and a little goes a long way with this. It also makes a great base for homemade tartare sauce or sandwich fillings.

4 egg yolks (75ml)

1 clove of garlic

1 tsp Dijon mustard

10ml white wine vinegar

10ml sherry vinegar

Sea salt

400ml grapeseed oil

50ml extra virgin olive oil

50ml extra virgin rapeseed oil

½ lemon, juiced

Place the egg yolks, garlic, mustard, both vinegars, and a pinch of sea salt into a food processor and whizz to combine. Combine the oils in a measuring jug and slowly trickle them into the processor as it blends. Once half the oil has been incorporated, stop the processor and squeeze in the lemon juice. Continue to blend the mixture while adding the remaining oil until it has all been incorporated, then season to taste. If the mixture splits, whisk in a tablespoon of iced water by hand to recover it.

AIOLI

MAKES APPROX. 350ML

Yes, it is a lot of garlic. We have the legendary London restaurant St. John to thank for this one, which is basically the ultimate garlic mayo. This is half the amount of garlic from the original recipe! Delicious, but probably best to sleep alone after heavy consumption.

300ml extra virgin rapeseed oil
10 cloves of garlic, peeled
3 egg yolks (45ml)
½ lemon, juiced
A pinch of sea salt

Measure the oil into a jug that's easy to pour from. In a food processor, blitz the garlic to a paste. With the processor running, add the egg yolks and let them combine for a minute. Very slowly, trickle in half the oil, then stop and add the lemon juice and sea salt. Start whizzing again and add the remaining oil very slowly. Season to taste and store in the fridge for up to 2 weeks.

BREAD SAUCE

SERVES 6

My Christmas guilty pleasure; this might be the thing I consume the most over the festive period. Truffle oil is optional, but it does add serious luxury to this very English condiment. Bread sauce can be made in advance, but you will need to add more milk when reheating for the right consistency.

500ml whole milk
2 shallots, peeled and halved
6 black peppercorns
2 bay leaves
12 cloves
2 thick slices of sourdough bread
100ml double cream
½ tsp nutmeg, freshly grated
Sea salt, to taste
2 sprigs of thyme, leaves only
30ml white truffle oil (optional)

In a large saucepan, heat the milk with the shallots, peppercorns, bay leaves, and cloves until steaming. Allow to simmer for 15 minutes, then remove the aromatics with a sieve. Blitz the sourdough to a coarse crumb in a food processor. Add the breadcrumbs to the milk along with the cream and nutmeg, then season with salt. Cook until thick, then add the thyme leaves and white truffle oil if using. Serve warm.

CUCUMBER RELISH

MAKES ROUGHLY 150G

A lovely spicy relish to have lying around in the fridge. I love this with fresh crab meat, as the balance of sweetness and spice with the fragrance of the fennel seeds is a perfect companion for sweet fresh crab. The relish is also great in summer salads or even with a chicken terrine.

50ml cider vinegar

50g soft brown sugar

1 tsp fennel seeds

1 cucumber, grated

½ green chilli, deseeded and finely chopped

1 shallot, peeled and finely diced

1 clove of garlic, grated

Heat the vinegar, sugar and fennel seeds in a pan on a medium heat until the sugar has fully dissolved. Turn the heat up and let the mixture just begin to boil, then remove from the heat.

Place the cucumber in a piece of muslin cloth and squeeze as much moisture out of it as you can. Tip the cucumber into a mixing bowl and stir in the chilli, shallot and garlic, then pour over the still warm vinegar mix and stir thoroughly. Leave to cool and season to taste, then store in the fridge.

HOUSE VINAIGRETTE

MAKES 300ML

This is a particularly versatile salad dressing that we have knocking around for a number of uses. Quick and easy to make, it will keep in the fridge for up to three months and serve you well across a bountiful summer salad season.

150ml extra virgin olive oil

50ml extra virgin rapeseed oil

50ml basil oil

50g Dijon mustard

75ml white wine vinegar

1 large clove of garlic, grated

½ lemon, juiced

Sea salt

Mix the oils together in a measuring jug. Whisk the mustard and vinegar together in a mixing bowl and once they are combined, begin to trickle in the oil, whisking continuously to emulsify the two mixtures. Finally, add the grated garlic, lemon juice, and sea salt to taste. Store the vinaigrette in a container suitable for drizzling and keep in the fridge for up to 1 month.

DIRECTORY

I've created this directory as a useful go-to for those wishing to buy better ingredients to enjoy at home. Most of these are suppliers that we use here at The Pack Horse, and a lot will help you discover some of the more unusual ingredients used in the recipes throughout this book.

MEAT

Mettricks Butchers
Local family-run butcher based in Glossop, High Peak. Exceptional quality, seasonal High Peak lamb. Our main butcher.
www.mettricksbutchers.com

Swaledale Butchers
Fantastic Yorkshire-based butcher specialising in rare breed heritage meats of the highest quality, aged in a Himalayan salt chamber. The breakfast sausages are a personal favourite.
www.swaledale.co.uk

Herb Fed Poultry
Yorkshire free-range poultry farm specialising in slow grown chickens and turkeys reared on a unique herb diet. The only chickens we ever buy.
www.herbfedpoultry.co.uk

Packington Pork
High welfare, free-range pork from a Staffordshire farm working towards net carbon-zero, powered by its own solar farm.
www.packingtonfreerange.co.uk

The Wild Meat Company
Suffolk-based online butcher specialising in local game meat of all varieties when available, arriving oven-ready and prepared to be used straight away.
www.wildmeat.co.uk

Holme Farmed Venison
Prime venison from sustainably sourced wild deer reared naturally in the countryside and traditional parks across the UK. Our chief venison supplier throughout the year.
www.hfv.co.uk

Cobble Lane Charcuterie
Based in Islington, Cobble Lane are among the finest producers of British cured meats, from authentic salamis to an English nduja. The Islington saucisson is a must try.
www.cobblelanecured.com

FISH

Pesky Fish
An online live fish market where you can purchase direct from the fisherman's boats. Total traceability from fishermen committed to low impact fishing methods.
www.peskyfish.co.uk

Wright Brothers
Extensive selection of seasonal fish bought directly from Brixham market.
www.thewrightbrothers.co.uk

The Cornish Fishmonger
Top quality, sustainable fish boxes caught from around the coasts of Cornwall.
www.thecornishfishmonger.co.uk

The Port of Lancaster Smokehouse
Experts in smoked fish from mackerel to salmon, and excellent sustainably sourced kippers and Morecambe Bay potted shrimps.
www.lancastersmokehouse.co.uk

OTHER INGREDIENTS

Forage Box
Online shop for seasonal wild ingredients including mushrooms and coastal vegetables.
www.foragebox.co.uk

The Mushroom Emporium
The finest Peak District grown mushrooms, available as fresh, dried, or grow your own in a box.
www.mushroomemporium.co.uk

Sushi Sushi
Specialists in Asian ingredients ranging from spices and sauces to dashi concentrates – cupboard staples that we rely on.
www.sushisushi.co.uk

Sous Chef
Stockists of specialist store cupboard ingredients ranging from artisanal oils and vinegars to restaurant quality stocks.
www.souschef.co.uk

Hodmedod's
Pioneers of British grown pulses, seeds and grains, bringing UK grown lentils to the mass market with a keen eye on sustainability.
www.hodmedods.co.uk

Peak District Pantry
Peak District-based online seller of seasonings, salts and hampers as well as quick meals to go, perfect to make over a camping stove.
www.peak-pantry.co.uk

Hartington Cheese Shop
Peak District-based cheese producers with their own little shop. The Dovedale Blue is a must try.
www.hartingtoncheeseshop.co.uk

The Courtyard Dairy
The experts in British cheese, supplying some of the nation's best restaurants and curating the finest cheeseboards.
www.thecourtyarddairy.co.uk

Nelstrops
200-year-old family-run millers based in Stockport blending their heritage and knowledge with modern methods to make the finest English flours.
www.nelstrop.co.uk

Doves Farm
UK market leaders in organic flour, alongside an excellent range of gluten-free flours and ancient grain alternatives.
www.dovesfarm.co.uk

Peak Bean
Artisan coffee roasters based in Hayfield, hand roasting ethically sourced beans and creators of our own in-house blend at the pub.
www.peakbean.co.uk

ACKNOWLEDGEMENTS

It has taken the best part of a year to bring this book together, but its story began here at The Pack Horse seven years ago. I'd like to thank my family for this. I've been so lucky to live in such a beautiful place and create my dream here, and it has meant the world to me to do it all with you. Firstly, Mum, for the initial help and getting everything up and running with us. It's been some journey we've shared together, and none of it would've been possible without you. Dad, for your constant mentoring, perspective, and relentless drive to support us in any way you can. Our conversations are invaluable and precious, both insightful and scattered with humour; I'm proud to have you as my guiding light. And of course, Emma, for believing in me right from the start, for sharing my vision for this incredible place and building it together over the years. You've seen me at my best and worst, and you're the only person I could ever run this business with. Thank you. And thank you for your sacrifices to raise Elliot, our beautiful boy. It may not always feel like it, but I am so grateful for you and your patience; you are a wonderful mother to our son who brings endless, much needed joy into our lives.

To our wonderful team past and present at The Pack Horse, thank you for being a part of the journey and shaping this pub into a truly special place. I cannot thank you all enough for your tireless hard work throughout the years.

A special mention has to go to Paul Chojnacki, not only for your help with the photoshoots for this book, but for always finding me the time to get the work done despite the challenges involved. I couldn't ask for someone better at my side. Also to Pedro Rolim, our kitchen engine, always on form and always there for the team. You are and always will be a special part of The Pack Horse family.

Thanks to those others who have dedicated their time to this book: Matthew Daniels, Jodie Morgan, Amy Brooks, Gabby Lee, Matthew Fearnley and Jack Currington.

To all our suppliers past and present – thank you for sharing your hard work and brilliance with us. We are nothing without you. Mettricks Butchers, Swaledale Butchers, Holme Farmed Venison, Herb Fed Poultry, Cobble Lane Cured, Sailbrand, RG Morris, Wellocks, Organic North, The Mushroom Emporium, Harvey & Brockless, Hartington Creamery, and all those others who have helped along the way.

Dan Burns of Natural Selection Design, how could I possibly thank you enough for this project? I knew it had to be you to photograph and help design this book as soon as I knew it was happening. Your creativity and talent are limitless, and I am so thankful to have you share the vision and dedicate so much of your time and energy to this book.

Thanks to David Dunford at Walks From The Door for helping to map the walking routes and provide the framework of the route instructions. You saved me a lot of time! Thanks also to Rob Whitrow for providing the additional photography required when the weather called for it.

To Meze Publishing, thank you for giving me this incredible opportunity to realise a dream. All your hard work throughout the editorial and design process has been immense; thank you all so much.

And lastly, to you. Our guests. Whether you've bought this book, visited the pub once, or are one of our village locals, none of this is possible without you. Your support throughout the last seven years has been mind-blowing, and I am eternally grateful for it. I look forward to seeing you again soon.